THE REFERENCE SHELF   VOLUME 37   NUMBER 2

RECREATION IN AMERICA

EDITED BY
PAULINE MADOW

THE H. W. WILSON COMPANY
NEW YORK   1965

THE REFERENCE SHELF

The books in this series contain reprints of articles, excerpts from books, and addresses on current issues, social trends, and other aspects of American life, and occasional surveys of other countries. Six numbers, comprising a volume, are published in each calendar year. One number is a collection of recent speeches on a variety of topics; each of the others, devoted to a single subject, gives background information and discussion from various points of view and concludes with a comprehensive bibliography.

Subscribers to the current volume receive the books as issued. The subscription rate is $12 ($15 foreign) for a volume of six numbers. Single numbers are $3 each.

23857

PREFACE

The word "recreation" means having fun or enjoying a pastime or diversion. It also means the various pastimes or diversions—the forms of recreation—themselves. Traditionally their purpose has been to refresh, or "recreate," the individual after a hard day's work. But the nature and function of recreation are changing in twentieth century America. Thanks to automation, generally rising prosperity, and a burgeoning population, it is no longer necessary to work from dawn to dusk in order to support oneself and one's family. With the shorter workweek and the shorter workday, there is more leisure for the majority of people than there was a generation ago. Hence there is more time for recreation, which has become increasingly not just a means of refreshment and relaxation at the end of the day, but also an activity to be explored, enjoyed, even "worked at" for its own sake.

The articles reprinted in this volume contain information and varied comments on the social and economic effects of increased leisure in America and on the role of public agencies in providing recreational facilities. In addition, some popular American pastimes are discussed. The last section examines the developing profession of recreational management and reviews various private agencies offering leisure-time opportunities.

The editor wishes to acknowledge her indebtedness to the authors and publishers who granted permission to reprint materials included in this compilation, to staff members of the National Recreation Association who extended many courtesies, and to the public information divisions of the Department of the Interior which supplied data and documents.

PAULINE MADOW

April 1965

CONTENTS

I. CHANGING PATTERNS OF LEISURE AND RECREATION

EDITOR'S INTRODUCTION

Nearly two thousand years ago Aristotle wrote that "if every tool when summoned, or even of its own accord, could do the work that befits it . . . then there would be no need of either workers by masters or of slaves by lords." Automation and modern industrial methods alone cannot produce the social and economic structure that Aristotle envisioned, but they have already had some far-reaching effects. Among these is the gradual but steady decline in working hours which is changing our attitudes toward both work and play. In recent years the ways in which we use our leisure have been the subject of comment and discussion by social critics expressing many points of view. A representative sampling of opinion is presented in this section. Much as the writers may differ, they all seem to confirm Bertrand Russell's observation that "to be able to fill leisure intelligently is the last product of civilization."

In the first article Bruce Bliven traces the expansion of leisure time in America and comments on its uses. Lest we become too optimistic, the next article summarizes the views of Sebastian de Grazia, author of the study *Of Work, Time and Leisure,* who maintains that the amount of leisure actually available to the average man is scarcely more than what it was a century ago. A business executive, a drama critic, and a philosopher speculate in turn on the prospect of ever-increasing leisure. Paul Goodman's article touches on class differences in attitudes toward leisure and deplores our inability to make adequate use of it. Nels Anderson analyzes the problems of the elderly involuntarily "at leisure." Margaret Mead discusses the work-leisure behavior pattern.

Full appreciation of the modern attitude toward leisure requires an understanding of the traditional attitude, which received its classic statement in Thorstein Veblen's *The Theory of the Leisure Class,* first published in 1899. With a good deal of irony at the expense of all sectors of society, Veblen held that the rich set the fashion for recreational activities and that men in each economic group follow the example of those with more wealth in order to share in their prestige. The section closes with an extract from his celebrated book.

THE RECREATION EXPLOSION [1]

A hundred years ago, the average workweek in the United States was about seventy hours. Today, it is about forty hours— and experts say that in the next decade or so it will be cut again, the predictions ranging from thirty-seven hours or thereabouts down to twenty or even less. This reduction might come as a shorter workday, or fewer workdays per week or longer—very much longer—vacations. . . .

In the last few decades, leisure has brought about a profound alteration in the patterns of our society, . . . A hundred years ago, nearly everybody worked very long hours, six or seven days a week, and family vacations were almost unknown. Rich men might send their wives and children to the seashore or the mountains in the summer, but rarely joined them for more than a few hours a week at most. Poor people, the overwhelming majority, had no vacations—their free time consisting of holidays of one or two day's duration.

Men and boys went hunting and fishing, but this was more to get food than as recreation. On special occasions like the Fourth of July, there were athletic events like wrestling, three-legged races or chasing a young greased pig, but many watched and few participated. It is hard for us to realize that most of today's organized sports go back less than a century—except horse racing, which has been practiced since antiquity. Baseball did not really take hold in its present form until the 1850's, football and tennis

[1] From "Using Our Leisure Is No Easy Job," by Bruce Bliven, author and former editor of the *New Republic.* New York *Times Magazine.* p 18-19+. Ap. 26, '64. © 1964 by The New York Times Company. Reprinted by permission.

until the 1870's, and golf and basketball until the 1890's. At the turn of the century golf and tennis were still considered the sports of the rich because of the cost of the equipment needed.

Today, we are seeing an astonishing "recreation explosion." We spend from $30 billion to $40 billion annually, perhaps as much as twenty times more per capita than we did in 1900. Max Kaplan, in his book, *Leisure in America,* reports that in 1959, 33 million people went swimming at least once, fishing was enjoyed by 32 million, dancing by 32 million, bowling by 18 million, hunting by 16 million. Baseball, professional and amateur, regular or softball, is played by 18 million, golf by 8 million and tennis by 4 million.

Other forms of outdoor recreation have also mushroomed. Skiing had not reached the United States in 1900, and water-skiing and scuba-diving had not been invented, but now millions participate in these sports. We spend more than $100 million annually on fishing and hunting licenses, and $1 billion on gardening equipment, seeds and plants. . . .

Spectator sports have expanded similarly—far beyond the increase in population. Kaplan says that 28 million watch baseball annually, 23 million football, 18 million basketball and 9 million horse racing. While hardly a sport, television is of course the most popular of all types of passive recreation. In less than two decades, it has grown to the point where people spend seven eighths as much time watching it as they spend at work! Last year, Americans occupied nearly 300 billion person-hours in front of the screen—or at least, with their sets turned on.

Not only has recreation expanded enormously, but it has been upgraded culturally. In 1900 there were 10 symphony orchestras in the country; today there are about 1,200. We have more than 1,500 local theater groups, most of them amateurs. People spend $500 million annually on concert tickets. In 1934, 500 records of Beethoven's Ninth Symphony were bought, and in 1954, 75,000. . . . Twenty million of us play the piano, 4 million the guitar, 3 million the violin. There are 2 million "Sunday painters."

We buy more than a quarter of a billion paperbacks each year. True, many of them are at the level of the pulp magazines of a generation ago, but they also include almost every classic there is and in editions many times larger than ever sold before. Though much of television is mediocre, its audience is so huge that the good things it offers have a fantastic impact. A single performance of *Hamlet* on a national network, for instance, reaches more people than all the performances in theaters from Shakespeare's day to our own!

Sixty years ago, very few employers paid any attention to what their workers did in their spare time, though some did arrange an annual "company picnic." Today the picture is wholly changed. Many big firms maintain vacation retreats and often they provide playing fields for their employees. The Scrooges who ran most of the big companies in 1900 would be aghast at the universal coffee breaks today—sometimes guaranteed by union contracts.

This increase in leisure and leisure-time pursuits has been made possible by the expansion in productivity per man-hour, which has trebled since 1900. Coupled with the growth of population, this has multiplied the production of goods by six times—which is lucky for us. As Gerard Piel, publisher of *Scientific American*, points out, if we were now turning out goods for a 1900 standard of living, we should have about 58 million unemployed. Looked at another way, we could maintain our present standard of living and still have 27 million unemployed if we worked the sixty-hour week common at that time.

One important difference, however, is that in those days work was usually more satisfying spiritually. People were craftsmen who gratified their creative impulse by beginning something and carrying it through to the end. Today, in contrast, most work is fragmented. The man or woman on a beltline performs one operation over and over again and the clerical worker has usually become a cog in a big impersonal machine. Many students of human behavior believe that this change has led to profound frustration, and that the character as well as the amount of recreation today represent an attempt by the individual to restore his psychological balance.

Georges Friedmann, a noted authority on the psychology of labor, believes that the character of work creates the character of play. Erich Fromm, the psychiatrist, thinks that the "do-it-yourself" movement, on which we spend $6 billion a year, has grown partly out of the yearning by today's workers for the exercise of a craftsman's skill. Indeed, he goes even farther and says in his book, *The Sane Society*: "The mode of work is itself an essential in forming a person's character."

Ferdynand Zweig, another labor expert, believes that modern factory work creates a great yearning to get "back to nature," the sort of impulse that sends so many people camping in the mountains, and jams our national parks to bursting point every summer. Daniel Bell, the Columbia University sociologist, thinks that the great impersonal modern corporation sets up in its employees a profound, if frustrated, desire to become one's own boss.

Despite the obvious advantages of the tremendous flowering of leisure activities in recent years, however, students of human behavior fear that people simply will not know what to do with themselves if the work week is still further reduced. . . . "Work," says David Riesman, the Harvard sociologist, in *The Lonely Crowd*, "is considered more important than play." . . .

Not until 1918 did the National Education Association pluck up enough courage to declare that learning good use of leisure was one of the cardinal aims of education. As late as 1926, the president of the National Association of Manufacturers could say, according to Harvey Swados in *Mass Leisure,* "I regard the five-day week as an unworthy ideal. . . . It is better not to tamper with God's laws."

Among those who flout "God's law" least are top business executives. While the general workweek is about forty hours, they average fifty-five—sixty hours. [Sebastian] de Grazia says that two thirds of them habitually take work home from the office. Half the industrial workers in the country now get three weeks' vacation annually, but this is not true of their bosses, who in theory could take as much time off as they pleased. Kaplan reports a survey which found that only a quarter of them took a month off, while one third took three weeks and another third, two weeks. The remaining one twelfth, presumably, were like George Bernard Shaw, who boasted he had never taken a vacation in seventy years.

Instead of adjusting in a relaxed fashion to the shorter work week, we seem to be going in the other direction. It is a commonplace to say that Americans "work hard and play hard," and that we don't know how to sit still and do nothing. Our tempo has speeded up to a feverish pace—Riesman says that we even play Bach and Mozart 10 per cent faster than was usual in their lifetimes. . . .

Some authorities feel that the pressure, which extends even to children, can do much harm. Professor Ronald C. Doll of Hunter College recently reported that children are expected to "be busy all the time," increasing the danger in later life of "heart attacks and nervous breakdowns." "When," he asks, "does the child have an opportunity to grow privately, quietly and independently to be himself?" This situation is characteristic of what Riesman calls the "other-directed" society, in which conformity to what someone else wants for you is the great objective.

What would people do if they had more leisure? Not necessarily what they say they would do. Business executives usually complain that they wish they had more time for reading and for cultural pursuits in general, but in fact they spend 80 per cent of their free time watching television or pursuing hobbies that can be called cultural only by stretching the term.

When large numbers of people were asked what they would like to do if they had more time, the biggest proportion said they would do more work around the house, and the second biggest, that they would spend more time with their families.

This agrees pretty well with their actual performance. When a typical sample was checked as to their most recent activities, it was found that after the omnipresent television, watched by about three fifths of the total, some two fifths just "visited" with friends or relatives, and one third worked around the house and garden (many of course did two, or all three, of these things). Discouraging to the uplifters is the fact that self-improvement with lectures or classes engaged only one in a hundred—the same proportion that went to a play or concert.

Does labor really want a shorter workweek? Riesman reports, in the symposium, *Mass Leisure,* that when a sample of trade-union members was queried, the rank and file seemed much less interested than their leaders. Riesman thinks this is because their leaders are better educated and have wider interests. (It is also true, of course, that they hold their jobs by making more and more demands on management—including a shorter week!)

In some parts, of the country as many as one third of the labor-union members said that if they had shorter hours they would go out and get a spare-time job to help meet expenses. It is a startling fact that about four million Americans are already engaged in this "moonlighting." . . .

Among both blue and white-collar workers, many mentioned that more time off would mean more "honeydew" days. These are days when your wife calls you to endless disagreeable chores with requests that always begin the same way: "Honey, do you mind cleaning out the playroom?" "Honey, do you want to take out the garbage?"

Is the prospect of greatly increased leisure as perilous as the prophets of gloom predict? Clearly, it needs to be carefully explored. We should have a great national debate on this subject, from the local level up to Congress. I don't feel, however, that there is any need for panic. We have already survived a doubling of our free time in the past few decades, and the adjustment has been made so readily that most of us are hardly aware that we have had one. Change will be rapid in future, but it will not come overnight. The American people are highly adaptable, much less bound by convention and tradition than those of most other countries, and we have powerful weapons of mass communication that can be mobilized when necessary.

Viewed in the long perspective, it is ironic, if not fantastic, that easing the burden of toil should be viewed as a problem and not as a blessing. Since time immemorial, men's lives have been constricted by the need for exhausting labor, as they still are in many parts of the world. We should rejoice that technology is now freeing us from that burden.

LEISURE—FACT OR FICTION [2]

The workweek is a great deal shorter than it has ever been. Vacations are longer. The auto and the airplane enable us to get places faster than ever before. Laborsaving appliances as well as frozen and prepared foods make it possible to do household chores in a fraction of the time it took our grandparents. Never, it would seem, have people been in such a favorable position to have and enjoy leisure. So why does the husband complain of the perpetual rat race? Why is mother exhausted by 6 P.M.? Why is nervous tension one of our leading health problems? In short, where *is* all the leisure?

This is a subject that has received plenty of discussion in car pools and garden clubs. But only recently has anyone done a scholarly research job to try to resolve the paradox. It was done by Professor Sebastian de Grazia [professor of political science, Eagleton Institute of Politics, Rutgers—The State University; author of the book *Of Time, Work, and Leisure*] under the auspices of the Twentieth Century Fund, and the conclusions are startling. Professor de Grazia finds that the great gain we think we have made in free time is an illusion. We're working nearly as hard as our great-grandparents did one hundred years ago— nearly as hard as the pioneers did when they settled in the West. And the so-called free time we do have is far from the classical concept of leisure. In fact, the generation of one hundred years ago, with all their long hours and lack of conveniences, probably went at a more leisurely pace than we do.

[2] Reprint of "Spare Time? *What* Spare Time?" *Changing Times.* 18:18-20. My. '64. Reprinted by permission from *Changing Times,* the Kiplinger Magazine, Copyright 1964 by The Kiplinger Washington Editors, Inc.

Why "Free" Time Isn't Free

Start with the official figures that show the workweek has shrunk from nearly 70 hours in 1850 to less than 40 hours today. In theory, we have acquired 30 shiny new hours each week to do with as we please. In addition, the increase in vacation and holiday time, if spread over 52 weeks, adds another $2\frac{1}{2}$ hours a week, making a total of around $32\frac{1}{2}$ free hours gained. The first fallacy here, according to Professor de Grazia, is that the 40-hour-week figure includes part-time work. If only full-time workers were covered, today's real average workweek would be around $46\frac{1}{2}$ hours, which cuts down our free time gained to only 25.

Then there's moonlighting. It has never been measured accurately, but it's undoubtedly very widespread, especially in industrial centers. In Akron, Ohio, for example, it is estimated that 16 per cent to 20 per cent of the rubber workers hold a second full-time job, while another 40 per cent hold down a second part-time job. Professor de Grazia figures that, on the average, moonlighting takes away another hour of theoretical free time, bringing the total gain since 1850 down to 24 hours.

Now how about commuting? In 1850 most people lived in rural areas or small towns where a man could walk to work and be there almost as soon as he finished breakfast. Today, nearly two thirds of the population live in urban areas where it takes a long time to get to work and home again. In the big cities rush-hour traffic flows at an average of 20 miles per hour for motorists and 13 miles per hour for public transit systems. Most people, however, either don't consider this to be part of their work time or else they tend to underestimate the total time consumed. One study showed that workers, on the average, use 45 minutes going to work and another 45 going home. If travel time to moonlighting jobs is included, then about $8\frac{1}{2}$ hours a week are used to get to and from work, bringing the free hours gained since 1850 to less than 16.

What about do-it-yourself work around the house? That generally comes under the heading of free-time activity, but Professor de Grazia points out that it is actually a way of paying for services in working time rather than in money. If such work is classified as part of our free time, he says, why do we consider that the pioneers had such a hard life? After all, the husbands and wives who settled the West spent practically all their time on do-it-yourself projects with a little hunting and fishing thrown in. If do-it-yourself projects are free-time activities, then the pioneers had nothing but free time.

Five hours a week is what Professor de Grazia allots to work around the house. This do-it-yourself work, he says, was not done in the 1850's. The skill required was too great, the materials too hard to work with, and not enough time was available. In addition, relatively few families owned their own homes, and for those who did, labor costs were so low that it paid to hire the work out. Thus, our weekly gain in free hours has dwindled to 11.

This isn't all. In 1850 when the man of the house was working 70 hours a week, his wife would hardly dare ask him to change the baby or dry the dishes. But today things are different. A great many wives are working. This, paradoxically, shows up in statistics as shortening the workweek. Thus, if a man works 48 hours a week, and then his wife gets a job working 35 hours, this further reduces the officially reported workweek and adds to the theoretically amount of free time, even though the family is working a total of 83 hours.

Remember, too, that these working wives call on their husbands for help. And the custom of husbands helping out apparently has spread even to families where the wife does not hold down a job. On the average, men put in nearly $2\frac{1}{2}$ hours a week on household chores, housekeeping and shopping, exclusive of the preparation of food. This leaves, of the $32\frac{1}{2}$ free hours a week theoretically gained since 1850, only $8\frac{1}{2}$.

And not all of these can be categorized as free. Moving from one city to another requires time for getting oriented in a new place. In certain kinds of work, a good deal of business is done during the lunch hour. These encroachments cannot be measured precisely, but they reinforce the argument that over the past hundred-odd years we have actually gained only a few hours a week of really free time.

And So We Feel Trapped

In part, this explains the trapped feeling that men and women complain of. There really isn't free time if by "free" we mean time to do just exactly what we want without any requirement or compulsion. When you ask people what they would do with a few more hours of free time a week, the typical reply is that they then could get more chores done—shopping, taking the children to the dentist, replacing the weather stripping. Thus, most of us, even if we had more "free time," would still be caught in the rat race. We would have no more leisure in the classical sense, which, according to the ancient Greek meaning, is an activity done simply for its own sake, such as listening to music, or just contemplating.

Excluded from this definition of leisure, in Professor de Grazia's view, are such activities as giving constant low-level attention to the movies, TV, radio and printed matter—all of which prevent a person from being alone with himself or "hearing from himself." Also excluded are recreational activities, such as bowling, which are primarily designed to refresh and "recreate" a person so that he will be in shape to go back to work.

This definition of leisure may seem somewhat ethereal in our modern world. But even so, who will deny that most of us habitually feel that we're on a merry-go-round or a treadmill, that we have no time to relax, that we're more and more afflicted by nervous tension?

This brings up the question, why haven't we used our laborsaving machines to give us the leisure we claim to want? Professor de Grazia's answer is in two parts.

First, our economic and political goals call for full employment, which has as a corollary an increasing flow of consumer goods and services. To keep the goods moving requires the most persuasive kind of advertising. Such advertising succeeds by purporting to prove that to save time, have more leisure and achieve the better life, a family need only purchase the growing variety of goods and services offered. But in order to make these purchases, the consumer must work harder and harder, moonlighting, allowing his wife to get a job, fixing the house himself to save money, and so on. Then as he acquires the goods, he must use them— watch TV, listen to the radio, mow the lawn with the power mower, make holes with the electric drill, water ski, and so on. The good life, where the consumer wears "leisure clothes" and participates in "leisure activities," such as skimming along in a $3,000 motorboat or a $4,000 car, is held out before him like the carrot before the donkey. But in the process of trying to obtain and enjoy this so-called leisurely life, he achieves not leisure but more hard work, more of the rat race.

Tyranny of the Clock

As the second part of his answer to the dilemma, Professor de Grazia blames the clock. The universal adherence to clock time is a fairly recent development. It came in with the factory.

Previously, work was done at home or near the home. The artisan was a relatively free man. His shop gave onto a well-traversed street in the town. He could leave his bench, table or lathe to go to the door to watch a passing procession. Afterward he could take up with a friend to go to the tavern for a drink. Work would wait until evening or the next day. He was not a slave to the clock during his working time, much less during his free time. Only the wealthy could know the correct time and even they considered their watches as toys.

The factory and the universal use of the clock changed all that. A man had to arrive at work at a given time to avoid wasting other men's time and machine time. Therefore he had to get up, shave, and eat and leave the house at a definite time. The clock's presence everywhere gave rise to the idea that workers were selling time as well as, or rather than, strength and skill. People began to speak of "spending" time rather than of "passing" time.

Gradually, the regulation of activities by means of precise time intervals spread to afterwork activities. Now, with a precise measurement of hours, minutes and seconds, all activities can be scheduled, and most of them are. The train leaves at 7:08, our turn at the tennis court is from 10 to 11:30, the meeting is at 8:15, the TV show starts at 9:30. All appointments must be kept by continual reference to the clock. The fear of being late, the nervous apprehension of not getting everything done in the time allotted, contribute to the tension. To be really free, time cannot constantly be clocked.

Will We Ever Break Free?

What's the solution? Can we break the hold the clock has on us, slow the production-consumption merry-go-round?

Someday, as a nation, we may do it. We may sour on our high valuation of production and efficiency. We may come to agree with Professor de Grazia that all great ideas have come from men who, although they may not have had wealth, had leisure. The philosophers, starting with Socrates, Plato and Aristotle, the great theologians, musicians, poets and, not least, the men who founded our own republic were men of leisure. As a nation we need such men. And as individuals, we need leisure for ourselves. Ask the housewife at 6 P.M., or the husband who, after commuting home from a hard day at the office, is reminded that the nominating committee of the PTA meets at eight o'clock sharp.

AUTOMATION: OPPORTUNITY OR DISASTER [3]

We are on the verge of a revolution in the production of time by automation. . . . What will be the future impact of automation on work? No one knows, but a few imaginative people are guessing. John Diebold, one of the young prophets in this new field,

[3] From *Inventing the Future*, address by Ralph Lazarus, president of Federated Department Stores, before the Family Service Association of America, San Francisco, November 16, 1963. Federated Department Stores. 222 W. Seventh St. Cincinnati, Ohio 45202. '63. Reprinted by permission.

wrote an article . . . for *McCall's* [July 1963] to which an excited editor attached this headline: "When Will Your Husband Be Obsolete?" In it Diebold predicted that within the next generation the work of 60 million Americans is "practically certain to be obsolete." And last summer a mathematician, admittedly pulling the figure out of thin air, told a press conference that within what he called "finite time" we should be able to produce all the goods and services we need with 2 or 3 per cent of the work force.

If we work with known facts, we need to make only a few fairly conservative assumptions, in my opinion, to reach the conclusion that our economy is going to provide us with substantial blocks of spare time in the next fifteen or twenty years. Between 1900 and 1940 technological advances allowed us to reduce the workweek by one third, or from 60 down to 40 hours. [For a different view of this change, see the preceding article.—Ed.]. . . Though we have slowed the pace of turning productivity gains into greater leisure since 1940, it seems to me we shall soon have to quicken it again because of the pressure from scientific research and development—commonly called R & D. . . . The Government alone has multiplied its commitments for R & D spending more than five times since 1955 and last year it obligated $15 billion, or 15 cents out of every tax dollar for this purpose. C. W. LaPierre, executive vice-president of General Electric, made this statement recently in an unpublished talk:

Over half of the nation's R & D expenditures since 1776 have occurred in the past seven or eight years. Very little of this latter half is yet reflected in our output. The development-to-use cycle is longer than that. Thus, our great technologically ingenious nation has hanging over it perhaps more discoveries yet to be applied than those that made it great. These technological discoveries are pouring out at an ever-increasing rate and are bound to have a major impact upon almost every human activity.

These discoveries will produce countless new products and new jobs, but their impact on working time is sure to be considerable. If we were able to cut working time by one third during the first forty years of this century, it should now take us fewer decades to repeat the performance. One third of a working life is more than fifteen years. It therefore seems to me that a reasonable hypothesis on which to proceed is that by, let us say, 1985, we should have accumulated at least a decade of disposable time per person.

Let us skip over the intervening years now and take a look at life in 1985. . . . The first thing to think about is our attitudes toward nonwork, for by 1985 automation may have forced our nation to turn leisure from a luxury into a virtue. We are automatically repelled by such an idea. It runs directly counter to the work ethic, which was rooted in our culture as far back as the third chapter of Genesis, when the Lord threw Adam out of the Garden of Eden. He condemned man to eternal labor in these memorable words, "In the sweat of thy face shalt thou eat bread."

Work has been integrated into man's moral code since the beginning. . . . Only when . . . tasks were organized with real efficiency could more than 10 to 15 per cent of any society live at much above the starvation level. This has been true up until the last five minutes of history.

This country was built on the Puritan belief that honest toil was the foundation of character, the cement of society and the uphill road to progress. Idleness was a sin. . . .

As a result, we treat free time today as a conditional joy. We permit ourselves to relax only as a reward for hard work or as the recreation needed to put us back into shape for the job. The aimless, delightful play of children gives way in adult life to a serious dedication to golf, the game that is so good for business.

Because of these attitudes, the prospect of having additional time off in blocks large enough to add up to a disposable decade is greeted with a reaction that is far closer to fright than to eagerness. To our guilt about idleness is added a fear akin to that of unemployment. Unemployment no longer brings starvation, but it does threaten that a life built around work could be robbed of meaning. It is an awesome prospect that the new leisure might force us to search for the meaning of life within ourselves. . . . To be liberated from the prison of work has been a consuming desire of man ever since he learned to write down his dreams. "The wisdom of the scribe cometh by opportunity of leisure," says

Ecclesiasticus, "and he that hath little business shall become wise."

Leisure was a passion to the Greeks, as we all know. . . . Perhaps the leisure of Greek life seems to us to be slightly un-American. If so, let us skip forward two millenia in time, hopping warily over the Puritans, and land in Philadelphia right in the midst of our own Periclean Age, the era of Jefferson. We find that glorious product of colonial leisure in the second-floor parlor of a house at Seventh and Market Streets writing these words: "We hold these truths to be self-evident, that all men are created equal, that they are endowed by their Creator with certain inalienable rights, that among these are life, liberty and the pursuit of happiness."

"The pursuit of happiness" was not just the whimsical phrase of one man; it went through all the re-drafts of the Declaration without change. It was central to Jefferson's complex philosophy. John Adams did not consider it even a novel political theory. "Upon this point all speculative politicians will agree," he wrote, "that the happiness of society is the end of government, as all divine and moral philosophers will agree that the happiness of the individual is the end of man". . . . Jefferson's faith got lost somewhere in the nineteenth century. What emerged out of the night of Victorian materialism was Josh Billings' definition of happiness: "Most of the happiness in this world konsists in possessing what others kant git." The Greek concept of leisure appears to be no more useful to our contemporaries than the Jefferson idea of happiness. . . .

We have to be thinking of a decade of disposable time, according to my guess, by 1985 or a decade and a half within thirty years. This is a third of a working lifetime. We do not know, of course, how this free time will be divided up among our occupations. The presumption is that common labor will be hit first and that free time will move upward and sideways through the skills on an unpredictable and erratic basis. The cynics say that those who have the lowest capacity for using free time constructively will get the most and that [highly trained] people . . . will actually have to work longer hours, since the demand for highly educated talents will far exceed the supply. But those who are bemused by the decision-making potential of the computer feel that some areas of middle management may face this problem, too. In any case, whether automation turns out to be an opportunity or a disaster, we must make sure that its effects are distributed equitably. . . .

We must, therefore, free our imaginations enough to devise new forms for time away from regular jobs. The one that opens the most attractive horizons seems to be the sabbatical year. This, strangely enough, is an American invention, devised some seventy years ago but available as yet only to professors. Its purpose is to give them every seventh year off for study, travel and renewal. . . .

I suspect . . . that most of us find a new purpose in life most easily through what we do. And once we shift our sights as a people, we will find plenty to do. All around us there are mountains of unfinished business to tackle. . . .

How much time and energy would it take to beautify our central cities and produce an atmosphere for living that would bring back the vast middle class? And what about our slums? The other day in New York I listened to a radio interview with a Puerto Rican who was describing the rooms in Harlem in which his family had been living, including the rats, the holes in the ceiling and the pipes that had been leaking steadily for five years. The general attitude on the program was that you can't fight City Hall. Can you imagine what would happen to City Hall if 10,000 sabbatical man-years were turned loose against it?

How much time and energy would it take to transmit the knowledge and technical skills that would enable the underdeveloped countries to abolish poverty, disease and ignorance so that they can secure for themselves their own versions of the better life? How much will it take to bring the neglected hordes of our own people up to the scale of health, wealth and education that we call the American way of life?

How many man-years of patient skill will we need to reverse the tide of school drop-outs for those who are capable of absorbing further education? What would happen if we decided to stockpile parks, forests and other recreational facilities ahead of the time we will actually need them and ahead of the time when they will be gone forever?

There is no end to unfinished business. Our education can be expanded in quality, quantity and variety way beyond the hopes of our most visionary pedagogues. That we should do this is, in fact, the sternest commandment of the coming era of automation. The speed of change and the growing complexity of both knowledge and the world will force us to extend formal education throughout life in order to keep up with the demands of new and old occupations, starting with science, technology, medicine and foreign affairs. And, far more difficult than that, will be the reorientation of education in the earlier years from its primary emphasis on preparation for life to preparation for living. . . .

The character of the living process has hardly been touched in recent years. We have done a relatively good job of insuring domestic tranquillity in the state within the meaning of the Constitution. But how much domestic tranquillity do we have in the family? How much serenity do we have in our lives? And how important is this to the future of the state? I agree with David Riesman that there can be a surfeit of things but that the market for intangibles and the people who produce them is truly insatiable. . . .

And so I come back to Jefferson's concept of the pursuit of happiness. It was a central concept of the American Revolution, whose real meaning was not freedom from something but freedom for something. It was centered on man, not on the state. It was freedom for man to fulfill his ancient promise. This he has done, at least in part, by building a paradise of plenty. Let us now pick up the gauntlet where Jefferson dropped it in 1776 and use this plenty as the opportunity to fulfill the rest of the promise. Let us now start to build a home fit for the human spirit.

THE MAN OF LEISURE NEEDS NO ADVICE [4]

Ever since the New Deal decreed the forty-hour or five-day week to discourage the Depression, intellectuals have been worrying about the leisure of other people.

Symposiums (okay, symposia) have been held to discover ways of preventing the masses from dissipating free time, and books have been authored (even publishers love that solecism) to elevate the lower orders to constructive use of idleness. The problem of enjoying leisure is still shot through with anxieties, and the most learned instruction comes from intellectuals who thrive under pressure.

In a recent article in the London *Observer*, Kenneth Tynan proposes a Ministry of Leisure to supervise the new leisure classes. "No one has yet come forward with a concrete plan for filling the new horizons of leisure," he says. He is really using leisure as a club with which to beat the government into giving more money to the arts. But he is aware of other crises. "Suppose I live in a region that has mountains but no mountaineering school," he supposes. Well, he could remain in the valley or he could get a map and compass and set out on his own.

Mr. Tynan has not had a moment to spare since he became England's most stimulating drama critic. Now on the staff of Britain's National Theatre, he is an ardent, versatile and useful citizen, and this column does not mean to be querulous about him. But it would like to ask him how he would feel if someone insisted that he cultivate leisure away from his chosen way of life. Probably he would have a nervous breakdown. Deprive him of ideas that incite him to action, bar him from the theaters, snatch away his books, forbid him attendance at public discussions, keep him off the platforms where ideas are being promulgated or refuted and he would be like Bernard Shaw dragged unwillingly by his wife on a cruise around the world. He would lock himself in his cabin and write something irascible, and the Ministry of Leisure would denounce him as a renegade.

[4] From "The Man of Leisure Needs No Advice on How to Spend His Free Time," by Brooks Atkinson, New York *Times* columnist and former drama critic. New York *Times*. p 32. Mr. 24, '64. © 1964 by The New York Times Company. Reprinted by permission.

The dictionary defines leisure as "time free from employment." More than five million Americans are now entirely free from employment. In fact, they are unemployed. They are probably demoralized because their lives lack purpose and direction. Unfortunately, this will become a more serious problem as automation eliminates more and more people from manufacture and commerce.

In the foreseeable future, automation will reach the point, R. Buckminster Fuller [engineer, architect, and inventor] declares, where "we are going to be completely unemployed as muscle-working machines. We, as an economic society, are going to have to pay our whole population to go to school and pay it to stay at school." Mr. Fuller, who cannot be dismayed by anything, looks forward to this with something approaching delight.

But it will not be leisure. It will be an advanced form of regimentation, which is just the sort of thing leisure should escape. Leisure is a form of private enterprise. Leisure is the time when a man can indulge in the sort of things that interest him personally. The man with leisure thrust upon him can listen to music or go to the theater if he wants to. Or he can pack up the wife and kiddies in the car and exhaust his nerves by creating traffic jams all over the landscape. . . . The man of leisure needs no advice from his betters.

In his leisure time, he will be not only happier but also more productive if he is left to his own devices. Organizing leisure time is the surest way of making a chore out of it. "Leave it alone," as conservationists say when someone presents a plan for improving nature. "Eat ye everyman of his own vine, and every one of his own fig tree." Or just sit under the fig tree. That would be a very high form of leisure.

WORK AND LEISURE [5]

Many anti-American cartoons abroad depict Uncle Sam brandishing a dollar as a symbol of American civilization. There

[5] Reprinted with the permission of Charles Scribner's Sons from *Reflections on America*, p 155-8, by Jacques Maritain. Copyright © 1958 Jacques Maritain. Mr. Maritain is a French Catholic philosopher.

is more ignorance than malice in this platitude. As a matter of fact, it is not money, it is *work* which holds sway over American civilization.

Everybody is working, and working hard. In this sense all are fundamentally equal, as working people (and people burdened by mortgages and deferred payment systems) who work to make a living, and who, after their daily hours, busy themselves again with any kind of task—handicrafts, improving their houses, sometimes building them, as Dr. Butterfield did, who was so sorry to leave his frame house, entirely built by him, when he became president of Wesleyan University. And they are more proud of their hobbies than of their jobs.

American civilization thus lays stress on the dignity of work and the fecundity of work transforming matter and nature. These are basic verities, in spite of all the fuss that the modern age is making about them—verities that essentially matter to man and society, and which ancient civilizations more or less ignored.

Yes. And for all that the fact remains that a certain boredom is caused by the absolute primacy of work and the disregard for the human value of leisure. Here is the dark side of the picture.

Let us think of the American attitude toward time. There is here, it seems to me, a certain horror of any span of time which a man might have at his own disposal in order to *do nothing*. The great value and efficacy of standing idle, and lingering over one's dream, is little appreciated in this country. One might wonder, for instance, whether committee meetings and all similar periodically recurrent administrative nuisances have not been invented to prevent professors, once they have finished lecturing, from having any time for idleness—that is to say, for thinking at leisure and pursuing their own research.

Well, friendship requires a great waste of time, and much idleness; creative thinking requires a great deal of idleness. So it is that leisure constitutes a serious problem for American life, especially given the social and technical progress, the automation, for instance, which makes working hours shorter and shorter in industry.

The question will be to have leisure time occupied in a manner really profitable to man, and not entirely taken up by the sort of stupefying passivity that is more often than not developed by movies or television. As long as a new cast of mind does not develop, involving a certain amount of spiritual epicureanism, the quality of leisure in the modern world will not be on a level with the quality of work.

If it is true, as Aristotle and Thomas Aquinas thought, that man cannot do without a certain amount of delectation, so that when he is deprived of spiritual delectations he passes over to carnal ones, how be surprised that all over the modern world the mass of humanity tamed by the general boredom of mathematized labor, should, if no superior flame is kindled, naturally become a prey to the obsession of sex (here the phenomenon, while taking especially pedantic forms, . . . has its external or symbolic expression in a curious return to a Greek nostalgia for the figure of Venus).

No leisure time will be enough for man to experience the joys of knowledge, of art and poetry, of devotion to great human causes, of communicating with others in the dreams and anxieties of the mind, of silently conversing with himself and silently conversing with God.

Work, which is a fundamental necessity of our existence, is not an end in itself. We work in order to improve human life. But will this very improvement, in ourselves and in others, only consist in working again and working more? Or will it also consist in the attainment of some superior possession, in which we shall rest? There are many kinds of rest. Laziness is sin. Amusement is good, but less good than work. Certain kinds of repose, in which the mind is supremely active, and reaches, however imperfectly, some fruition of immortality through its contact with truth, or with Eternal Love, are better than work.

Higher forms of leisure are no longer leisure but act come to completion. And the highest form is contemplative activity. *Be still, and know that I am God* (Psalms, 45:11 Vulgate).

LEISURE: PURPOSEFUL OR PURPOSELESS [6]

The Greeks had a word for leisure, σχολή, meaning serious activity without the pressure of necessity; and another word, διατριβή, which meant playful amusement to pass the time, and both were excellent things. Serious leisure was the chief way that a free man grew in character and a city in culture. And pastime was the recuperation from serious pursuits, including leisure. . . .

For some of our old-fashioned social thinkers, like Bertrand Russell or William Morris or Edward Bellamy, this very prospect of our modern leisure was always bright and promising; it aroused the hope that modern man could again turn to a high leisure-culture, like the Athenians of antiquity, and make our great technological adventure pay off historically, the automatic machines being our slaves. . . . These philosophers forget that the Athenians worked at their leisure with deadly earnestness; that, quite apart from their slaves and their empire, they earned their leisure by being content with a fantastically low standard of private life for all classes, and got their deep satisfactions from patriotic service and civic culture. American life is not frugal; it is less and less political or patriotic, and our notion of community is restricted to philanthropic contributions; and, of course, our economic life makes it impossible for us to work earnestly at our leisure. Thus, far from offering a hope of culture in the Greek style, or of the art of living in the old Japanese style, our mass-leisure threatens us with a terrifying problem, namely that people with all that surplus time will goof off and get into trouble.

When the sociologists discuss mass leisure, they are not talking about serious activity at all, nor are they talking about culture and relaxation. Their concern is a simple one: how to save the millions of people with long hours heavy on their hands from fooling around or being drowned in canned entertainment and spectatoritis; how to provide something for them which is an activity, has some dignity and does not disintegrate personality.

[6] From "The Mass Leisure Class," by Paul Goodman, author and educator. *Esquire.* 52:70-2. Jl. '59. Reprinted by permission of Esquire Magazine. © 1959 by Esquire, Inc.

To quote a succinct remark of Russell Lynes, "In the simplest terms, the primary problem of leisure is how to avoid boredom."

His solution: give people a planned, purposive activity, like learning to be a connoisseur of working with a "do-it-yourself kit." (Just think of it! These categories, of fooling around vs. planned purposive activity, were precisely those that a philosopher, John Dewey, used to stress as important for the pedagogy of *children*. One is dismayed to see grown-up sociologists satisfied to apply them to grown-up human beings.)

The result is an odd, American kind of view of leisure. There's activity free from the pressure of necessity, but it *must by no means be vitally important to the individual or the nation;* for that would disrupt our work-leisure pattern, confuse our motivational hierarchy, disturb family life, and interfere in politics. Is this not powerfully reminiscent of a dilemma of the WPA in the days of the Great Depression? If the unemployed were given useless jobs, called boondoggling, it was considered morally bad for them; but if they were given useful work, like the excellent WPA Theatre, then they were in competition with private enterprise and that was disapproved. . . .

America at Work and at Leisure

Nearly all the writers—seldom does one read such a consensus —here speak of the disaster of the Calvinist Ethic. Their argument runs as follows: since the Americans were brought up to believe that only hard work is righteous and that playtime must be earned and designed to make them fit for more work, now in easier times they find it difficult to enjoy themselves. But this makes no sense, for the problem is not that Americans don't enjoy their leisure, but that there's little *in* it to enjoy. A good time is not, and cannot be, a goal; it is always the blessed accompaniment of some successful, vital activity. Furthermore, the Calvinist Ethic is essentially true. If a man doesn't give himself without timidity to a real effort that satisfies his best standards of honor, integrity, and utility, he *is* not in a state of grace. How many men have such jobs? Few.

In this respect women are much better off. The housewives of a Westchester suburb play cards for an average of two hours every weekday. The ladies have fed their families, gotten them off to school and work, cleaned up and bought supper, and taken care of the baby: all this is honorable endeavor, unquestionably useful, and justified. When they sit down with the other "girls" for their sociable game, we can be sure they are placid about it, and play well too. But the men in the same milieu have to dream up purposive do-it-yourself activities.

Like the women, the plain working stiff, who has a job without prestige, is better off than the more pretentious employee, for when he is at leisure his mind is free of the job. But what is the job and what is his work attitude? When we answer this we see why serious leisure is impossible at present in America.

In a little study of industrial workers, a sociologist named Robert Dubin set himself to study the attitudes and choices of the men at a plant in order to find means to cement the loyalty of the men to the organization. Using psychological questionnaires to test their evaluations on three issues he found: (1) For a thumping majority, as an important life interest, the job left them cold. "They found their preferred human associations and preferred areas of behavior outside of employment." (Therefore, Dubin concluded, the employer might as well give up trying to make the work as such more attractive, for the workers couldn't care less.) *But* (2) even though they didn't give a hoot about the job, for a good majority of the men, their notions of how to behave correctly in life, how to be accepted, how to succeed, how to give orders and obey, *were* job-oriented, toward the rational, impersonal organization and its staff; their normative standards of behavior did *not* come from family, friends, or community. And (3) in their choices with regard to technique, efficiency, quality of material and equipment, cleanliness, accuracy, carefulness— all the things that we would consider as part of a man's craftsmanlike and aesthetic capacity—again a good majority proved to be oriented, not to sports, not to home economics and do-it-yourself, not to arts and crafts, but to the job at the plant.

The Problem of Our Leisure

Reflect on what those findings mean, unsurprising as they are, and you will understand the problem of our leisure. What the men are *really* interested in is the time off the job; they are just waiting for the whistle to blow so they can get to their "important" interests; but, strangely, those important life interests are *not* directive, controlling, rewarding; they are *not* the areas of learning how to belong and how to avoid being excluded. Such things are rather learned on the job, in which, however, they are not interested! Also, the men do not respect the form or technique that they might spontaneously develop in their off-time interests; that's all bungling; the arts are for . . . girls; sports are just fights. The dance of life, they believe, is correctly and seriously performed only on the job, in which they are not interested. But, then, what on earth can be the quality of home or leisure activities where there is no belief in their righteousness or their style? The leisure activities *must* lack daring, confidence, and invention; they must be . . . conformist, herding together for security and trying to have a good time without asserting oneself. In fact, they are American mass leisure.

And with whom will one have the good time? The possibilities seem to be people one meets on the job, or in the community, or old friends, or one's family. Dubin's findings rule out comrades from the job. Other studies demonstrate the obvious proposition that no one has a good time with members of his family. In America we have no community relations to speak of. (This was, by the way, the great advantage of the Greeks, that it was their city that gave them confidence in their rightness and style.) This leaves us only friends, friends with whom one has no vocation in common, no sexual or paternal relation, no political or community enterprise, no deep respect for one another's skill or authority. It is, of course, not much to go on.

My own hunch is that for very many the most rewarding leisure moments are those spent alone, especially if one has the excuse of seeming to be occupied, . . . Driving in the car alone, sitting in the bar with a glass of beer, or pretending to be busy with a magazine or hobby or do-it-yourself, but really passing in and out of fantasy. This is a pathetic picture, but not lacking in warmth. As for the workingman, he spends his sunny holidays "fixing the car." This is obviously useful and money saving, and not uninteresting in itself; and it is a connection with the machine that gives freedom to go, to get away. Only he does not much know *where* to go, so he goes to the movies—and parks the car outside.

White-Collar Leisure

If we now skip up a class or two in prestige, the work-leisure pattern is psychologically more desperate. The industrial worker is not hung up on the job and he has the comfort and protection of the union. But the white-collar worker, the salesman, the technician, the junior-executive are committed organization men. Their work is demanding and actively engages the mind, and their position is esteemed as important. So their orientation toward the job is not only strong, but it overflows into off-time. The organization dictates the right clothes, the right conversation pieces, and often the right wife; and a man goes to sleep with his work problems. Salient, of course, is the need to compete and the fear of being displaced from eminence, with no recourse to a union. . . .

And white-collar leisure has the same complex tone as the job (unlike working-class leisure which is often different and disorderly). Though conforming to the approved behavior, nevertheless a man's performance must be individualized and expert, and, if possible, competitively One Up. His sport clothes and equipment are not bought from army surplus as good enough and durable; they must be bought for the fashion and the label. If he plays bridge, he uses conventions appropriate for champions, although they are less effective for an amateur than his own good card sense. He buys beautiful standard equipment to do-it-himself and he must end up with a product that looks standard. The result couldn't be otherwise. In the complexities he loses his creativeness.

Whether at golf or the expensive lunch on the firm or the barbecue in the patio, business and leisure are inextricably entangled. The tone must be having-a-grand-time-glad-you-are-here, but the undertone that is always there, that removes relaxation from leisure, is often ulcer-producing fear. . . . It is rarely that a man can apply to his organization his highest standards of honor, integrity, and utility, or say his best say, or use his best powers; a man is lucky if, in a thoughtful moment, he does not have a twinge of conscience and a sense of self-betrayal. One consequence of this is the common fantasy of a Flight to the Woods, which is a leisure activity pretty sharply restricted to this prestige group. "Wilderness travel," concludes a typical survey, "is an exclusive recreation. Education data confirm the high status of canoeists. More than half had either completed college or received graduate degrees. Only one respondent (out of forty-five) had not completed high school." In the Woods a man is again independent, pure, manly, simple, and accompanied by uncompetitive buddies or an understanding and sexy wife. But the equipment for the camping trip is bought at Abercrombie and Fitch, and the wife complains that she was roped in. . . .

Another, more global, response to their situation is to shrink from the real job altogether, and set up as commuters in a garden city or the near countryside and devote themselves to bringing up the new generation. Shall we call this a leisure activity or a kind of schizophrenia? There is no doubt that the New Fatherhood is an attempt by the man to horn in on his wife's occupation for, presumably, it contains some satisfactory reality. The bother with it is that when both parents devote themselves just to bringing up the children, the children do not have much of this wide, wide world to grow up toward.

Possibly the chief serious and worthwhile leisure that these persons do engage in is nonmedical psychoanalysis or other psychotherapy, which, in its peculiar way, is not very different from the ancient Socratic Conversation whose aim was to Know Thyself. We would phrase it, Find Yourself. This vital pursuit has immense mass-attractiveness in America, but it is unfortunately not mass-available because understaffed. . . .

The Distinguished Retirees

Jump a few more rungs up the ladder of prestige, and we come to the respected company of retired or semiretired businessmen and professionals who have made their mark and a lot of money. What do these distinguished oldsters, who used to work very hard, do with their now free time? . . .

Along with the mothers of grown children, their chief activity is likely to be community service, especially philanthropies; and they provide us with a jolly illustration of the work-leisure pattern in America. The actual casework in our community services, whether in nurseries, the needy, hospitals or the prevention of delinquency or prejudice, is of course severely restricted to experts; for both better and worse, an amateur do-gooder is kept out of contact with the raw facts of people. But our retired men of distinction are put to use in finance and administration, in fund-raising, in keeping the community chest, on building committees. Naturally this suits them perfectly; with their prestige, their skill in public relations, and their business acumen, it is just what *they* are expert at, it is what they have always done. The jolly part is the conviviality and spirit with which they throw themselves into it; some of them blossom and feel complacent for the first time in their careers. . . .

The Undistinguished Retirees

But let us go back to the dark hint we began with, that a lot of people are productively expendable altogether. In a surplus technology, many are retired before they have ever gone to work. What then becomes of the pattern of work-and-leisure?

It is astonishing that the social critics have not pointed out that this a major explanation of the phenomenon of the so-called Beat Generation. These illustrate the pattern of work-and-leisure when one of the terms has vanished; they are only at leisure. Critics, like [Norman] Podhoretz in the December 1958 issue of this magazine, are incensed that the Beat produce no cultural values and yet are paid attention to; but they fail to ask where the cultural and workmanlike standards of the productively surplus could possibly come from. Perhaps the valuable contribution of the Beat is that it forthrightly demonstrates the extreme of our problem of mass leisure. There is nothing *needing* to be done, and so they don't know what to do with themselves at all. They refuse to be tricked into behaving as though they were economically or culturally necessary, when they are patently not necessary. They refuse to make the effort to get the conventional leisure satisfactions, but satisfy themselves with sloth and quasi-visceral kicks. . . .

It is simply a mistake, springing from lack of acquaintance, to lump together the Beat and the juvenile delinquents as Podhoretz does. Naturally, since it does not participate, Beat has no positive cultural forms, and therefore picks up from other marginal groups, like Puerto Ricans, Negroes, thieves, and dead Japanese. But the Beat psychology is the very opposite of delinquent. Beats are not juvenilely rebellious, but often went through college and may now be in their later twenties and thirties. They grew up in families, on whom indeed they still sponge, maintaining embarrassed relations. Their desires, manners, and showdown behavior are rather blander than that of the average solid citizen. This is being cool; it is their way of not suffering. For they are displaced persons, born on the wrong planet. So they are at leisure. It is that inwardly they *cannot* identify with the values of father and his society, for they are too hip; yet on the other hand they cannot rebel against them, disregard them or transform them, for they aren't hip enough. After a while the present group will make some conventional adjustment. (Madison Avenue has some of them and will soon be chock-full.) But the present group will be replaced by another generation, for the problem is endemic. . . .

It is not with impunity that mankind misses its opportunities to make a brave new world, for after a while people no longer remember what it is to be serious in either work or leisure. Young people particularly are disillusioned when they learn that society's way of life is not authentic; and, ceasing to believe, some refuse to take part. For most men there is no man's work, and also therefore no man's play.

THE AGING, AGED, AND FORLORN [7]

Neither in work nor leisure is old age a matter of mere sentiment. With the extending life span, it amounts to about a tenth of one's adult years, if one lives much past seventy. [Seymour L.] Wolfbein notes that, whereas in 1900 one out of each twenty-five Americans was sixty-five or older, in 1950 one out of twelve was in that age bracket. . . .

The rejection of the old by the labor market, as [Clark] Tibbitts finds, begins for some workers before they are sixty-five, but some may continue active after that age. . . .

For the old to be negatively affected in work means also to be negatively affected in leisure. For the old as for other workers, status in leisure often reflects status in work. Although they have "earned a rest," their position with respect to leisure remains ambiguous, . . .

A Man and His Worth

At any point in his life the individual tends to be rated in terms of nonsentimental values: what he owns, his occupation, his work record, and the influence he wields. Perhaps the family name is considered. His worth from year to year may rise or fall. During his middle years it may remain for a considerable time at a given level. His worth curve begins in his youth, wavers as it rises to some high point and then wavers its way down.

Perhaps the same factors would be included in estimating a man's potential worth. . . . Other factors may also be considered: . . . social class, his "character," education and training, what he may have achieved. . . .

Both worth and potential worth are social as well as economic ratings. They concern the rating of the individual by others, but they also condition in one way or other his rating of himself. He may put forth considerable effort to hold his ratings up or to raise them, but as he gets older he knows very well that the ratings will decline. Not only does he know this, but he knows that

[7] Reprinted with permission of The Free Press from *Work and Leisure*, by Nels Anderson. First published 1961 by Routledge & Kegan Paul Limited. © Nels Anderson 1961. p 182-204. Nels Anderson is former director of the United Nations Educational, Scientific and Cultural Organization's Institute for Social Sciences, Cologne, Germany.

others are aware of it. His utility is not always determined on the basis of his ability to work; his age may be a more potent factor in the downward turning of his worth curve, and then he makes his exit from the labor market, retirement. He has time but he can no longer sell it. . . .

Old-Age Status and Security

Ours is perhaps the first civilization to invent retirement as a means of dealing with old age. . . . One can see the day coming, but he works on and then there is an abrupt stop.

The Council of State Governments' . . . report [*The States and their Older Citizens,* 1955] indicates: (1) a good share of the old people are in need, but (2) the situation is improving. And the report adds that many of the aged who have economic security meaning above the subsistence level, are still not happy because emotional security is lacking. They are in a sense outside of society, not linked with community life. . . .

So the old do not dominate the modern community . . . [as in] earlier societies, . . . they become instead a tolerated group. This applies only to the old who lack wealth or power. Actually, the modern society is dominated by the old in high places. It would be unusual in an international meeting of diplomats to see any men under sixty years of age. . . . Old men predominate among the most powerful leaders in business and industry, the same industries that dismiss workers at sixty-five. When people in such top-level posts retire, it is not a retreat to isolation. For most farmers and for most self-employed urbanites retirement, not only comes late, but it involves no future of loneliness. This is mainly the problem of the great majority who sell their time for wages or salaries, often those especially who have reared families.

[The report of] the Council of State Governments found that 27 per cent of the aged couples in the United States were living on an "emergency budget," which allows no money for leisure or comfort. Moreover, of the aged single persons, most of them widowed, 33 per cent of the males and 51 per cent of the females were living on such an emergency budget. What is pertinent there is that most of these old people complained of loneliness. Some, of course, were homebound because of physical or mental handicaps, but still more were apparently cut off socially, or had isolated themselves. Modern community life is such that one becomes automatically isolated when he ceases on his own initiative to be identified with it. It is true that various organized groups try to meet this situation by forming "golden age" clubs, which help, but not enough. Therefore "the number of isolated and lonely aging people in every community is many times as high as the number enjoying the sociability and fellowship of these clubs."

From Loneliness to Loneliness

If he did not know it before, once the individual retires he discovers that all the roles in which he figured to that point—spouse, parent, neighbor, friend, club member, citizen and so on—leaned heavily upon and revolved about his role as worker. The more dominant the role of worker may have been, the more helpless he is likely to be when one day he must leave work behind. If he has not already learned there are other ways to use time enjoyably, he must learn after retirement, if possible, for leisure also has values, and we quote [L. C.] Michelon ["The New Leisure Class," *American Journal of Sociology,* January 1954]:

Work ways and values	*Leisure ways and values*
1. When a person is busy at work and faced with daily problems, he is engaged in vital living. Problem facing and problem solving are what make life worth living. They lend to the development of personality.	1. The individual must now live for himself—to satisfy his own person rather than to worry about what a job or other people require of him.
2. The working person is important to others and then to himself—that is, he is a jobholder, family man, company man, etc. Work for a purpose, service to others, obligations—these are important conditioners of values.	2. New friends and a new community of interests must be substituted for the breakup of his work and home relationships.

3. Leisure is particularly good at that time because the time free from business is made satisfying by the knowledge that there will be a return to work—with its corresponding meanings to the individual.

3. The individual must come to see that what he formerly considered peripheral activities are the most important and most satisfying. He must see in them basic, substitute values for the meaning of work.

Married women seem to adjust more quickly to retirement than do married men, apparently because they need make no abrupt transition from everyday life. . . . Single women, particularly career women, seem to have as much difficulty in adjusting to retirement as professional men or businessmen. They also seem to have more difficulty than single men of the same age. Professional men and businessmen, on the other hand, are more reluctant to retire than the average workingman. And when they retire completely they have more difficulty in making a satisfactory adjustment.

When the meaning of work to the individual is positive, the transition to retirement is more difficult. When the meaning of work is negative or neutral the transition to retirement is easier.

On Wheels

Retirement for many Americans is an invitation to escape, to get out of sight, or perhaps to venture into experiences not possible before because there were too many obligations or too little time. If the individual has never developed the art of escaping in fantasy or to what [J. A. V.] Butler calls "imaginative participation in other kinds of lives," then he may find escape in a change of scenes, following the American tradition of moving somewhere else. . . .

In different ways the retired ones may "get away from it all," entering a type of retirement at present fashionable in the United States—traveling with a trailer pulled behind the automobile. . . . Hence the auto camps found outside every town and city, and the great auto camps outside urban places in the South. Florida, Mississippi, Arizona and California are among the mecca states for retired people traveling in trailers. Many, of course, go to these same areas to live in hotels, if they can afford it, or in cottages. [William H.] Harlan mentioned that in some Florida cities every fourth or fifth adult is sixty-five years of age or older. In such cities, business caters to the elderly, which is evident when one notes the health food stores, the drugstores, the hobby shops and the number of physicians specializing in the ailments of the aging.

Outside these same cities are the trailer camps, anywhere from a hundred parking places for trailers to camps of a thousand or more parking places. The voyager puts his trailer on a spot for which he pays rent. . . . He then connects with the electric power and water supply and housekeeping can begin. In the trailer camp will be stores, recreation hall, a movie and a post office. He may stay for weeks, or move again in a few days. The fact that one can move any time he wishes lends an atmosphere of freedom to this living, something not possible in those cottage communities some propose for the aged, isolating them in a sort of ghetto out of contact and out of sight. But in trailer camps:

Personal adjustment in retirement and old age is facilitated by the attitudes and institutional practices of mobile-home communities. Social roles which are congruent with the needs and interests of the retired person are sanctioned. The primary interests center around leisure and recreation. . . . The implementation of a central recreational program is, of course, greatly facilitated by the nature of the trailer park.

This opinion by [G. C.] Hoyt is based on a study he made of Florida camps. . . .

Of the men 61 per cent and of the women 52 per cent took part in camp activities: shuffleboard, cardplaying, pitching horseshoes, bingo, Bible class and hobby clubs, to mention the more important. He found much visiting and conversation, and "pot luck" group dinners were frequent. Hoyt found there was little contact between the retired in the trailer camp and the local community. The reason is that trailer people are not flush with money as tourists often are. . . .

The trailer camp is one sort of escape activity for retired people, although they may find it tiresome after a while. For

some, it may be helpful in getting over the first shock of retirement after which the elderly pair may return to a new version of
home life. . . .

Old Age and Life Enjoyment

In 1950 the National Conference on Aging expressed [in *Man
and His Years,* 1951] the view that too many Americans "reach
late life completely unprepared for the leisure" that retirement
may bring. Further regarding this emptiness: "Millions have but
seldom read a book, have rarely played a game, have taken little
or no part in community affairs. They have concentrated their
whole interests within the narrow confines of job and family, and
when these pass their lives seem desolate and empty. They find it
difficult to believe that they still have capacity for developing
new interests and relationships." . . . The idea of community
hardly exists, even for many actively employed. . . . People will
go on trying to stave off the signs of age when they will be out
of the commercial amusement market as well as the labor market.
The leisure industries make youth so glamorous that the prospect
of aging becomes something dreadful to contemplate, so people
resort to hair dye, elixirs, physical culture, take to modern dancing
and so on to keep up the illusion of youth. [Robert J.] Blakely
calls it the cult of youth: . . . "Our task is not just to restore old
people to participation in our society. It is also the integration of
the idea of growth, the essence of which is growing old, into our
philosophy." . . .

One explanation for the unhappy condition of many of the
American aged at the working-class grade has been their economic
dependence, their living at a subsistence level and looking to their
children for help. Once the aged at this economic plane are able
to live on their pensions not only will their relations with their
children and other relatives improve, but their community contacts will develop. Living at the poverty level tends to break such
contacts as the aged may have. As the Federal Security System
gets more favorably established in day-to-day thinking we can
expect a relaxation of those pressures which have operated so
effectively to keep pensions at a subsistence level. This may not

solve all the emotional problems of old people, but if they can feel sufficiently secure economically to maintain their self-respect they will go far in solving their own individual time-use problems. . . .

What needs to be understood is that, even if the old are no longer needed in productive work, and that will be more true in the future, they are needed in the life of the community. In every previous society they performed what might be called a balancing function. . . . They still have this function in our society, but the performance is limited to the very upper echelons of state, church, industry, the professions, labor organizations and so on. At the lesser levels they also have a function, if it is only to play with the children and sit on the sidelines while the young play the game. The old are not being utilized if they are pushed aside to find their laughter among the old. . . .

Apparently we are entering a phase of our social evolution when leadership is also needed in consumption, when work not for pay will gain importance. In such developments we already see emerging a new type of community life and to the balance of that life the old can make a contribution.

THE CONTEMPORARY PATTERN OF LEISURE [8]

Within traditional American culture, leisure is something that has to be earned and re-earned, except for the very old. Seen as play for the child, recreation for the adult, and retirement for the old, both child and adult have to earn their rights—the child by growing and learning, the adult by working. Unearned leisure is something which will have to be paid for later. It comes under the heading of vice—where the pleasure comes first and the pain afterwards—instead of virtue, where the pain or work precedes the reward. In some cultures, the joyful consumption of the harvest is felt as part of a natural climax structure; in others, the slightest feasting must be paid for later, almost as if

[8] From "The Pattern of Leisure in Contemporary American Culture," by Margaret Mead, curator of ethnology at the American Museum of Natural History, and author of many books and articles on culture patterns. *Annals of the American Academy of Political and Social Science.* 313:11-15. S. '57. Reprinted by permission.

it had been taken out of one's flesh. Within American culture, however, there has been a rhythm of work, virtue, and leisure. Good works—to be distinguished from work because they yield no monetary rewards and yet are enjoined and not enjoyed—are classified with work, and the Sabbath comes into more and more of an ambiguous position. . . .

The word *recreation* epitomizes this whole attitude of conditional joy in which the delights of both work and play are tied together in a tight sequence. Neither one may ever be considered by itself, but man must work, then weary and "take some recreation" so he may work again. The linkage effects both joy in leisure and joy in work. It is wrong to work too hard; to become deeply, obsessively interested in work, or good works; one *should* have some recreation. And the minute that it looks as if there would be more time in between work and good works than the amount needed for "healthy recreation," alarm spreads over the country. . . .

Unearned Gains

Experience of many different sorts has shown that the pessimists are right, that relaxations of this relationship between time spent in work and time spent in leisure do often result in boredom, apathy, frantic attempts to fill up the time, too much drinking, promiscuity, gambling, reckless driving, and so forth. Unearned gains are not moral gains, and so there is a tendency to spend them in ways which are labeled as immoral, or at least as idle luxury. In Elliott Jaques's study of an English factory, he found that men who were making more than they believed, on a nonverbalized level, to be fair were spendthrift. This was characteristic of World War I war workers in the United States, whose position was felt to be twofold unfair—they were safe from the hazards of the trenches and were paid too much for their work, such earnings going into silk stockings and fur coats. And Jaques found that workers who were paid too little, within their deep evaluation of what their job was worth, became apathetic and wished to leave their jobs. The whole system is like a bowstring. If overstretched or slackened, pathological effects result.

The answer which the last hundred years have attempted to give to the problems of a discrepancy between the time and effort involved in work, the available patterns of good works, and the traditional amount of pleasure which could go with them without strain has been the suggestion that people "take up something as a hobby"—that they should do something which is not serious, has no monetary value, and so will be of no use to anyone but oneself. It may, however, be "expensive," and so use up some discrepancy between earning and legitimate spending. It must be something which is somehow out of the value system, something neither good nor bad, neither quite work nor quite play, and which can therefore fall under the bridging concept of "recreation."

Toward a New Equilibrium

The period since World War II has seen a breakdown of this system of earned and re-earned limited pleasure. The Depression brought a slackening of the whole system. When people did not have enough work, no money, and so no symbolic right to play, entertaining was curtailed, movie money was short, dates lacked gaiety, childbearing was postponed. Work when it came back would bring with it a renewed ability and right to get some joy out of life. But World War II introduced a mixed set of disturbances. These included war workers who made too much money; soldiers who had too little time on leave and who spent too much time in absolute dullness and boredom overseas; men and women who saw too little of each other; families who still had to postpone their little modicum of privacy and live with relatives. After the war, there came, understandably, a desire to recoup these quantitatively perceived losses, to get some joy out of life. This was, perhaps, less because joy was a goal than because of the desire to reattain an equilibrium which had been disturbed since the lush, disequilibrated days of the late twenties.

Somewhere in the last decade there has come a subtle shift in this picture. This is a shift characteristic of our culture throughout its life and characteristic of most peoples who have depended on long hard hours of work for the majority in order that they should simply survive. Conditions which have contributed to this shift can only be sketched in very roughly. They include a rising standard of living; rising wages; creeping inflation; and ways in which the relationships between work done, money made, and what one can buy are continually threatened. They also include a lowered standard of work proficiency in almost all fields; high wages for adolescents who often make more than their parents; easy installment buying, so that a car is fully used up by the time it is paid for; and the threat that this prosperity will not last. Furthermore, there is the fear that there will be an atomic war, or at least a devastating depression produced by automation. These are the terms in which individuals are experiencing the rapid shifts in our economy. There is our emphasis on the importance of mass markets to keep up production, on improved standards of living in other countries as helpful rather than threatening to our economy, on the unlimited possibilities inherent in automation on the one hand and free power on the other. There is a freeing of men from drudgery of all sorts so that their potentialities may be utilized. This is a thing which has only been experienced before in occasional small societies under conditions of extreme and usually temporary felicity. Such opportunities have never been experienced for the large majority of the people of a great civilization.

The Shifting Balance

The generation which has married since the war has responded to these conditions by shifting the balance from work and good works to the home. The home, in which one was once allowed a limited amount of recuperation and recreation in reward for working hard, has now become the reason for existence, which in turn justifies working at all. This does not mean that many young people are not working very hard. Husband and wife often both work, combining work, children, and going on getting an education. But the emphasis is different. Jobs are selected as they will bear on the home. In the familiar phrase of how a man will account to his Maker for his life on earth, having been a good husband and father heads the list. Good works in the form of community service within the social environment right around the home have been moved into home life, as has most of religious participation. "I had to join some church so my son could be a cub scout." Hours of work which permit a man to spend more time at home, length of vacation, amount of strain and overwork, all are valued as to how they will affect family life. As once it was wrong to play so hard that it might affect one's work, now it is wrong to work so hard that it may affect family life.

But has family life become leisure in this process of transformation? Reversing a proposition within the kind of moral book balancing characteristic of our culture produces many complications. A great deal has been done to turn modern home life into a self-rewarding delight. It has become something that is neither work nor something done in order to make a living, nor recreation, that is, something done to get you safely back to work again. The do-it-yourself movement, which parallels so neatly the shortage of skilled labor for home finishing and repairs, is not just a hobby. It is often a pleasant and meaningful contribution to family life. The newfound delight of young fathers in their babies is another intrinsically rewarding pattern. . . . The gay companionship of a large family, making do with a small house, one car, and two dogs, has many ways of fending off boredom and apathy and the demand for expensive entertainment. The car, the television set, the pets are seen as contributory to the home. Service on innumerable boards and committees in the community is also part of making the community safe for the children.

But there are hazards inherent in the old work-play rhythmic morality which lie just beneath the surface of these readjustments. If this home life really is to be classified as play, then it should be a good deal easier than it is. For our notions of play have been those of spectator sports and easy enjoyment for a long time. Do-it-yourself with five children, besides being delightful, is strenuous, time consuming, backbreaking, nerve-straining, and confining—most of the things once characteristic of a good job which a man enjoyed. The job outside the home, if not seen as recreation in the spiritual sense, is becoming recreation in the physical sense. It is a relief from the exactions of the close personal life at home, a chance for a little peace and quiet, a quiet smoke, time to collect one's thoughts. The insidious old rhythm between enjoined activity and permitted brief limited relaxed behavior is reasserting itself. A girl goes to work until she marries, or after she marries, or after her children are in school as a supplement to the home. It is unfair of her employer to ask much of her work hours—as it would once have been unfair for him to infringe on her day off. If a man is doing the best he can, getting up at night with his young babies, taking them off their mother's hands as soon as he gets home, or perhaps getting supper because she has a part-time job too, it is unfair to ask him to wear himself out at work. As home life and personal relations thus take the center of the stage, the old rhythm remains with the job—less and less often a career—becoming the subsidiary, determined part of the sequence.

It is obvious that the whole question of *recreation,* which gives merely instrumental value to joy, needs a type of revision. This must be a revision which will make the members of a society—where delight in high-level proficiency should now replace dogged willingness to work long hours for very limited rewards—able to integrate the shorter hours of work and the new engrossing home rituals into some kind of a whole in which these outmoded sequences, heritage of an age of scarcity, can be overcome.

CONSPICUOUS LEISURE [9]

In order to gain and to hold the esteem of men it is not sufficient merely to possess wealth or power. The wealth or power must be put in evidence, for esteem is awarded only on evidence. And not only does the evidence of wealth serve to impress one's

[9] From *The Theory of the Leisure Class,* by Thorstein Veblen, American economist and social philosopher. Modern Library. New York. 1934. p 35-67. All Rights Reserved. Reprinted by permission of The Viking Press, Inc. (This work was first published in 1899.)

importance on others and to keep their sense of his importance alive and alert, but it is of scarcely less use in building up and preserving one's self-complacency. In all but the lowest stages of culture the normally constituted man is comforted and upheld in his self-respect by "decent surroundings" and by exemption from "menial offices." Enforced departure from his habitual standard of decency, either in the paraphernalia of life or in the kind and amount of his everyday activity, is felt to be a slight upon his human dignity, even apart from all conscious consideration of the approval or disapproval of his fellows.

The archaic theoretical distinction between the base and the honorable in the manner of a man's life retains very much of its ancient force even today. So much so that there are few of the better class who are not possessed of an instinctive repugnance for the vulgar forms of labor. We have a realizing sense of ceremonial uncleanness attaching in an especial degree to the occupations which are associated in our habits of thought with menial service. It is felt by all persons of refined taste that a spiritual contamination is inseparable from certain offices that are conventionally required of servants. Vulgar surroundings, mean (that is to say, inexpensive) habitations, and vulgarly productive occupations are unhesitatingly condemned and avoided. They are incompatible with life on a satisfactory spiritual plane—with "high thinking." From the days of the Greek philosophers to the present, a degree of leisure and of exemption from contact with such industrial processes as serve the immediate everyday purposes of human life has ever been recognized by thoughtful men as a prerequisite to a worthy or beautiful, or even a blameless, human life. In itself and in its consequences the life of leisure is beautiful and ennobling in all civilized men's eyes. . . .

Even if the institution of a leisure class had not come in with the first emergence of individual ownership, by force of the dishonor attaching to productive employment, it would in any case have come in as one of the early consequences of ownership. And it is to be remarked that while the leisure class existed in theory from the beginning of predatory culture, the institution takes on a new and fuller meaning with the transition from the predatory to the next succeeding pecuniary stage of culture. It is from this time forth a "leisure class" in fact as well as in theory. From this point dates the institution of the leisure class in its consummate form. . . .

The normal and characteristic occupations of the class . . . are government, war, sports, and devout observances. . . . At this as at any other cultural stage, government and war are, at least in part, carried on for the pecuniary gain of those who engage in them; but it is gain obtained by the honorable method of seizure and conversion. These occupations are of the nature of predatory, not of productive, employment. Something similar may be said of the chase, but with a difference. As the community passes out of the hunting stage proper, hunting gradually becomes differentiated into two distinct employments. On the one hand, it is a trade, carried on chiefly for gain; and from this the element of exploit is virtually absent, or it is at any rate not present in a sufficient degree to clear the pursuit of the imputation of gainful industry. On the other hand, the chase is also a sport—an exercise of the predatory impulse simply. As such it does not afford any appreciable pecuniary incentive, but it contains a more or less obvious element of exploit. It is this latter development of the chase—purged of all imputation of handicraft—that alone is meritorious and fairly belongs in the scheme of life of the developed leisure class. . . .

Leisure in the narrower sense, as distinct from exploit and from any ostensibly productive employment of effort on objects which are of no intrinsic use, does not commonly leave a material product. The criteria of a past performance of leisure therefore commonly take the form of "immaterial" goods. Such immaterial evidences of past leisure are quasi-scholarly or quasiartistic accomplishments and a knowledge of processes and incidents which do not conduce directly to the furtherance of human life. So, for instance, in our time there is the knowledge of the dead languages and the occult sciences; of correct spelling; of syntax and prosody; of the various forms of domestic music and other household art; of the latest proprieties of dress, furniture, and equipage; of games, sports, and fancy-bred animals, such as dogs and race horses. In all these branches of knowledge the initial motive from which their acquisition proceeded at the outset, and through which they first came into vogue, may have been something quite different from the wish to show that one's time had not been spent in industrial employment; but unless these accomplishments had approved themselves as serviceable evidence of an unproductive expenditure of time, they would not have survived and held their place as conventional accomplishments of the leisure class.

These accomplishments may, in some sense, be classed as branches of learning. Besides and beyond these there is a further range of social facts which shade off from the region of learning into that of physical habit and dexterity. Such are what is known as manners and breeding, polite usage, decorum, and formal and ceremonial observances generally. . . .

It is among this highest leisure class, who have no superiors and few peers, that decorum finds its fullest and maturest expression; and it is this highest class also that gives decorum that definitive formulation which serves as a canon of conduct for the classes beneath. And here also the code is most obviously a code of status and shows most plainly its incompatibility with all vulgarly productive work. A divine assurance and an imperious complaisance, as of one habituated to require subservience and to take no thought for the morrow, is the birthright and the criterion of the gentleman at his best; and it is in popular apprehension even more than that, for this demeanor is accepted as an intrinsic attribute of superior worth, before which the baseborn commoner delights to stoop and yield.

II. RECREATION AND PUBLIC POLICY

EDITOR'S INTRODUCTION

In the years following World War II, the demand for housing, highways, schools, airports, and factories led to unprecedented building activity that used up open land and other natural resources at an alarming rate. Government on all levels has responded to this development with plans and projects to broaden its role in the conservation and creation of resources both to preserve the shoreline and countryside and to meet the pressure of increasing recreational needs.

To determine the requirements of outdoor recreation in the next decades, the Outdoor Recreation Resources Review Commission (ORRRC)—headed by Laurance S. Rockefeller, composed of congressmen and private citizens, and aided by state officials and various experts—studied the situation for three years. Since the presentation of ORRRC's report, *Outdoor Recreation for America,* to the President and Congress in 1962, many of its recommendations have been carried out. These include creation of a Federal Bureau of Outdoor Recreation, addition of land and seashore areas to the National Park System, and enactment of provisions of the Watershed Protection and Flood Prevention Act (1962), Water and Land Conservation Fund Act (1964), Wilderness Act (1964), and Land Classification and Multiple Use Act (1964).

Further implementing the spirit of the ORRRC's report, President Lyndon B. Johnson pledged his administration to certain conservation and recreational policies in his State of the Union Message of 1965. "We must make a massive effort," he declared, "to save the countryside and establish—as a green legacy for tomorrow—more large and small parks, more seashores and open spaces than have been created during any period in our history." He spoke also of his intention to "landscape highways and provide places of relaxation and recreation wherever our roads run." (The Federal Government has already undertaken to finance in large part a 41,000-mile highway system, over which recreational travel is expected to exceed 50 billion miles each year.) Later, on February 8, 1965, the President detailed his program for outdoor recreation in a special message to Congress on natural beauty.

Besides recreation in the out-of-doors, the Federal Government is concerned with other leisure-time activities. For example, Congress enacted the Library Services Act of 1956 providing monies for expansion of library facilities over a five-year period and in 1961 extended the law for another five years. In a related area, Congress approved the Adult Education Act of 1962, authorizing funds for instruction of adults deficient in reading and writing skills. The Government takes an interest, too, in what is perhaps the most popular form of indoor relaxation: watching television. Its Federal Communications Commission (FCC) has regulatory authority under the standard of the "public interest, convenience, and necessity" over radio and TV transmission.

In addition, the Federal Government has played a major role in opening recreational facilities to all of its citizens. On October 20, 1958 the Supreme Court emphasized its position against racial discrimination in tax-supported facilities such as municipal parks, playgrounds, and golf courses. In 1964 Congress approved the Civil Rights Law, which prohibits racial discrimination in public accommodations, including restaurants, motels, and places of amusement that are involved in interstate commerce. This prohibition was unanimously upheld by the Supreme Court on December 14, 1964.

Another aspect of government operations affecting leisure time is the Social Security System. The system handles over $12 billion annually for benefits to older people, many experiencing enforced full-time leisure. (See "The Aging, Aged, and Forlorn," Section I, above.)

The first article in this section, excerpted from the ORRRC report, reviews the factors contributing to the greatly increasing recreational needs and suggests programs for meeting these needs.

The next two selections, by Secretary of the Interior Stewart L. Udall and President Johnson respectively, link the expanded need for recreational areas and facilities with the broader problems of conservation, control of air and water pollution, and urban planning. Next, another part of the ORRRC report examines the economic benefits that can accrue to an underdeveloped community through an outdoor recreational facilities program. The two articles that follow describe the Federal Government's Small Watershed Program and National Park Service. Another surveys different types of recreational programs and facilities provided by state governments. The final selection, an extract from a speech by former FCC Commissioner Newton N. Minow, discusses the Federal Government's concern with the principal medium that provides indoor recreation—television.

OUTDOOR RECREATION FOR AMERICA [1]

This report is a study of outdoor recreation in America—its history, its place in current American life, and its future. . . .

By 1958, Congress had decided that an intensive nationwide study should be made of outdoor recreation, one involving all levels of government and the private contribution, and on June 28 of that year it established the Outdoor Recreation Resources Review Commission.

The authorizing act, Public Law 85-470, set forth the mission. It was essentially threefold:

To determine the outdoor recreation wants and needs of the American people now and what they will be in the years 1976 and 2000.

To determine the recreation resources of the nation available to satisfy those needs now and in the years 1976 and 2000.

To determine what policies and programs should be recommended to ensure that the needs of the present and future are adequately and efficiently met. . . .

[1] From *Outdoor Recreation for America; a Report to the President and to the Congress by the Outdoor Recreation Resources Review Commission.* United States. Outdoor Recreation Resources Review Commission. Supt. of Docs. Washington, D.C. 20402. '62. p 1-74; 81-178.

The Demand

The demand is surging. . . . Barring a war or other catastrophe, it seems very likely that the population will virtually double—from about 180 million today to approximately 230 million by 1976, and to 350 million by the year 2000.

It will be a more concentrated population; compared to 63 per cent in 1960, about 73 per cent of the people will be living in metropolitan areas by the year 2000. There will be more young people. The proportion of those in the 15-24 age bracket—the most active of all—will go from the current 13 per cent of the total to about 17 per cent by 1976.

At the very least, then, these figures suggest a doubling of demand by 2000, even if participation did not increase. But it will. Studies of other trends indicate that in the years ahead the individual will be participating a great deal more in recreation than he does now.

Incomes, for one thing, will be higher. With a projected annual growth rate of gross national product of 3.5 per cent, disposable consumer income is expected to rise from $354 billion in 1960, to $706 billion by 1976, and to $1,437 billion by 2000. More people will be moving into the higher-income brackets. In 1957, about 14 per cent of the consumer units had incomes of $10,000 and over; by 1976, it is estimated the proportion will be up to 40 per cent and by 2000 to 60 per cent (in constant 1959 dollars).

With this new affluence, many more Americans will be able to afford the kinds of activities—like horseback riding, water skiing, and boating—that they do not do now but would very much like to do. As the economic base widens, furthermore, many of the present differences between groups in the kinds of recreation they seek will lessen. There will also be a shift in the occupational composition of the population, with more people in the professional, technical, and white-collar categories, and this is likely to bring about an increase in outdoor activity. And an expected increase in the educational level of the adult population may be felt in greater participation in such activities as nature walks, attending outdoor drama, playing games, and sightseeing.

People will have more free time. By 1976, it is estimated that the standard scheduled workweek will average 36 hours for the entire industrial work force versus 39 hours in 1960. And by 2000 it may be down to 32 hours. Much of the extra time will go to recreation; at least one fifth of free time goes into outdoor recreation today, and we may expect at least this much in the future.

The inclination is already quite evident. A large number of people report that they would like to engage in a great deal more recreation activity than they do at present. They cite lack of time as the chief barrier. Lack of money is next. As people get more of both, there will be a considerable step-up in per capita demand; and even a modest increase, when it is applied to a doubled population, could have a great multiplying effect.

The forecasts of travel suggest an enormous expansion. In air travel, for example, some 30 billion passenger miles were flown by domestic carriers in 1960; by 1976, the figure may reach 150 billion; and by 2000, it could go as high as 325 billion. The number of passenger cars is projected at 100 million by 1976—an increase of nearly 80 per cent above the number registered as of 1959—and by 2000 the number is expected to grow by as much again. The new degree of mobility should be impressive indeed, and among other effects, this will inevitably increase the pressure on recreation sites that now seem remote. . . .

Patterns of Demand

Equally as important as the magnitude of demand is the way in which it is distributed among the groups within the population. There are significant differences in the desire for outdoor recreation between young and old, rich and poor, city people and suburbanites. The groups themselves, furthermore, are changing—incomes are rising, the older are living longer. . . .

Of all the factors, age has the sharpest influence. As might be expected, the older people get, the less they engage in outdoor activity. This decline is especially noticeable in the more active pursuits—cycling, hiking, horseback riding, water skiing, camping. . . .

Income has a discernible effect upon the rate of participation. With activities that demand a substantial outlay of time or money —boating, water skiing, horseback riding, and the like—it is hardly surprising that participation is higher among those who have the leisure and resources to participate. Interestingly enough, however, the upper-income groups also do more walking.

Some of the differences between income groups are due to such related factors as education, occupation, and age. The very low rate of participation by the bottom-income group, for example, can be partially accounted for by the high proportion of older people, many of them retired, in this bracket. . . .

In the range of activities as well as the total, nonwhites engage in outdoor recreation less than whites. The nonwhite rate of participation is markedly lower in water sports and in camping and hiking; it is higher in playing games and walking.

Participation does not vary by sex as much as by age or income, but in total, men do tend to participate more than women—a difference largely due to the strong interest men show for such traditionally masculine pursuits as hunting and fishing. In activities like swimming, driving, picnicking, and camping, women participate as much if not more than men. A key fact about such activities, indeed, is that they are family activities.

Families seek outdoor recreation together. About 60 per cent of family heads (or their wives) indicate that the whole family enjoys at least two of the same outdoor activities. Families turn to activities in which children can participate along with the parents. The aspiration of parents to educate the child to a level above their own extends to helping him develop in outdoor pursuits.

Occupation has a considerable influence, though, to some extent, it may not be so much the particular work a man does as how much he is paid for it and how long a vacation he is given. Among occupations, professional people enjoy the most recreation, farmworkers, the least. The managerial and proprietor group is somewhat under the average for all occupations. This may be due to the large number—perhaps half—of self-employed in the group. In general, the self-employed and their wives show a lower rate of outdoor activity than others. Small entrepreneurs and retailers have to spend a lot of time minding the shop—and they do not get paid vacations. . . .

But for all the differences among groups, what is more significant is how alike they are. The demand is pervasive. About 90 per cent of all American adults engage in some activity in the course of a year. Thus, those involved are not just a small group of outdoor enthusiasts but the large majority of the American people. . . .

Some Findings of the Study

As results of the studies began flowing to the Commission, some old ideas were discarded, some were reinforced, and some new concepts evolved. The following are a few of the major conclusions.

Simple activities most popular

Driving and walking for pleasure, swimming, and picnicking lead the list of the outdoor activities in which Americans participate, and driving for pleasure is most popular of all. This is generally true regardless of income, education, age, or occupation. . . . It is something of a tribute to Americans that they do as much cycling and walking as they do, for very little has been done to encourage these activities, and a good bit, if inadvertently, to discourage them. We are spending billions for our new highways, but few of them being constructed or planned make any provision for safe walking and cycling. And many of the suburban developments surrounding our cities do not even have sidewalks, much less cycle paths.

Europe, which has even greater population densities, has much to teach us about building recreation into the environment. Holland is constructing a national network of bicycle trails. In Scotland, the right of the public to walk over the privately owned moors goes back centuries. In Scandinavia, buses going from the city to the countryside have pegs on their sides on which people can hang their bicycles. Car ownership is rising all over Europe, but in the planning of their roads and the posting of them, Europeans make a special effort to provide for those who walk or cycle.

Why not here? Along the broad rights-of-way of our new highways—particularly those in suburban areas—simple trails could be laid out for walkers and cyclists. Existing rights-of-way for high-tension lines, now so often left to weeds and rubble, could at very little cost be made into a "connector" network of attractive walkways. . . .

Needs of metropolitan areas

Three quarters of the people will live in these areas by the turn of the century. They will have the greatest need for outdoor recreation, and their need will be the most difficult to satisfy as urban centers have the fewest facilities (per capita) and the sharpest competition for land use.

Over a quarter billion acres are public-designated outdoor recreation areas. However, either the location of the land, or restrictive management policies, or both, greatly reduce the effectiveness of the land for recreation use by the bulk of the population. Much of the West and virtually all of Alaska are of little use to most Americans looking for a place in the sun for their families on a weekend, when the demand is overwhelming. At regional and state levels, most of the land is where people are not. Few places are near enough to metropolitan centers for a Sunday outing. The problem is not one of total acres but of *effective* acres.

Financing and planning

Most public agencies, particularly in the states, are faced with a lack of funds. Outdoor recreation opportunities can be created by acquiring new areas or by more intensive development of existing resources, but either course requires money. Federal, state, and local governments are now spending about $1 billion annually for outdoor recreation. More will be needed to meet the demand.

Fortunately, recreation need not be the exclusive use of an area, particularly the larger ones. Recreation can be another use in a development primarily managed for a different purpose, and it therefore should be considered in many kinds of planning— urban renewal, highway construction, water-resource development, forest and range management, to name only a few.

Most people seeking outdoor recreation want water—to sit by, to swim and to fish in, to ski across, to dive under, and to run their boats over. Swimming is now one of the most popular outdoor activities and is likely to be the most popular of all by the turn of the century. Boating and fishing are among the top ten activities. Camping, picnicking, and hiking, also high on the list, are more attractive near water sites. . . .

In the forty-eight contiguous states, the recreation shorelines of the Atlantic, Gulf of Mexico, Pacific, and Great Lakes total over 21,000 miles. Of this total, 4,350 miles are beach, 11,160 miles are bluff shores, and the remainder is marsh shoreline. The total shorelines of Alaska (33,904 miles) and Hawaii (1,092 miles) also offer a wide variety of recreation opportunities. . . . It is estimated that some 90 per cent of this limited, highly desirable resource is under private control, about 5-7 per cent is in public recreation areas, and about 3 per cent is in restricted military areas. . . .

Economic benefits

Although the chief reason for providing outdoor recreation is the broad social and individual benefits it produces, it also brings about desirable economic effects. Its provision enhances community values by creating a better place to live and increasing land values. In some underdeveloped areas, it can be a mainstay of the local economy. And it is a basis for big business as the millions and millions of people seeking the outdoors generate an estimated $20 billion a year market for goods and services. [See "The Recreation Explosion" in Section I, and "Economic Benefits of Outdoor Recreation," the fourth article in this section.]

Importance of outdoor recreation

About 90 per cent of all Americans participated in some form of outdoor recreation in the summer of 1960. In total, they participated in one activity or another on 4.4 billion separate occasions. It is anticipated that by 1976 the total will be 6.9 billion, and by the year 2000 it will be 12.4 billion—a threefold increase by the turn of the century.

As outdoor recreation increases in importance, it will need more land, but much of this land can be used, and will be demanded, for other purposes. Yet there is little research to provide basic information on its relative importance. More needs to be established factually about the values of outdoor recreation to our society, so that sounder decisions on allocation of resources for it can be made. More must be known also about management techniques, so that the maximum social and economic benefit can be realized from these resources.

Recommendations

The recommendations of the Commission fall into five general categories:

A national outdoor recreation policy.

Guidelines for the management of outdoor recreation resources.

Expansion, modification, and intensification of present programs to meet increasing needs.

Establishment of a Bureau of Outdoor Recreation in the Federal Government.

A Federal grants-in-aid program to states. . . .

A National Outdoor Recreation Policy

Implementation of this policy will require the cooperative participation of all levels of government and private enterprise. In some aspects, the government responsibility is greater; in others, private initiative is better equipped to do the job.

The role of the Federal Government should be—

1. Preservation of scenic areas, natural wonders, primitive areas, and historic sites of national significance.

2. Management of Federal lands for the broadest possible recreation benefit consistent with other essential uses.

3. Cooperation with the states through technical and financial assistance.

4. Promotion of interstate arrangements, including Federal participation where necessary.

5. Assumption of vigorous, cooperative leadership in a nationwide recreation effort.

The states should play a pivotal role in making outdoor recreation opportunities available by—

1. Acquisition of land, development of sites, and provision and maintenance of facilities of state or regional significance.

2. Assistance to local governments.

3. Provision of leadership and planning.

Local governments should expand their efforts to provide outdoor recreation opportunities, with particular emphasis upon securing open space and developing recreation areas in and around metropolitan and other urban areas.

Individual initiative and private enterprise should continue to be the most important force in outdoor recreation, providing many and varied opportunities for a vast number of people, as well as the goods and services used by people in their recreation activities. Government should encourage the work of nonprofit groups wherever possible. It should also stimulate desirable commercial development, which can be particularly effective in providing facilities and services where demand is sufficient to return a profit.

Guidelines for Management

All agencies administering outdoor recreation resources—public and private—are urged to adopt a system of classifying recreation lands designed to make the best possible use of available resources in the light of the needs of the people. . . . The following system of classifying outdoor recreation resources is proposed:

Class I—High-Density Recreation Areas: Areas intensively developed and managed for mass use. . . . They are particularly suited for day and weekend use. Although subject to heavy peak-load pressures at certain times, they often sustain moderate use throughout the year. These areas are generally located close to major centers of urban population, but they also occur occasionally within units, such as national parks and forests, remote from population concentrations. . . . Typical examples of Class I areas are portions of Palisades Interstate Park, New Jersey and New York; Jones Beach, New York; parts of the Cook County Forest Preserve, Illinois; Huntington Beach State Park, California; Patapsco State Park, Maryland; the beach and boardwalk area in Atlantic City, New Jersey; and the Colter Bay recreation center in Grand Teton National Park, Wyoming. . . .

Class II—General Outdoor Recreation Areas: Areas subject to substantial development for a wide variety of specific recreation uses. Their special feature is the ability through development of facilities to sustain a large and varied amount of activity, such as camping, picnicking, fishing, water sports, nature walks, and outdoor games. . . . These areas range in size from several acres to large tracts of land and are popular for day, weekend, and vacation use. . . .

Class III—Natural Environment Areas: Various types of areas that are suitable for recreation in a natural environment and usually in combination with other uses. . . . Typical recreation activities are hiking, hunting, fishing, camping, picnicking, canoeing, and sightseeing. In contrast to Class II areas, planning and development in Class III areas should emphasize the natural environment rather than the provision of man-made facilities. . . . Recreation developments on Class III lands should be limited to basic facilities that are in keeping with the natural features of each area. . . . Under this policy, commercial operations such as resorts, trailer parks, marinas, and entertainments would be excluded. Where provided, overnight facilities would be simple and in keeping with the natural environment.

Class IV—Unique Natural Areas: Areas of outstanding scenic splendor, natural wonder, or scientific importance. The scenic sites and features included in this class are limited in number and are irreplaceable. They range from large areas within Yosemite Valley and the Grand Canyon to smaller sites such as Old Faithful in Yellowstone National Park; Old Man of the Mountain, New Hampshire; the Bristle Cone Pine Area in the Inyo National Forest, California; and parts of Cape Cod. . . .

Unique natural areas should be preserved for inspirational, educational, or scientific purposes. General activities such as swimming, picnicking, motorboating, camping, hunting, and fishing should be excluded. Food, lodging, automobile service, and other facilities should generally be located outside the immediate area. Adequate access for the enjoyment and education of the public should be provided wherever consistent with the primary objective. . . .

Class V—Primitive Areas: Undisturbed roadless areas characterized by natural, wild conditions, including "wilderness areas." Size is a limiting factor only to the extent that the area must be large enough and so located as to give the user the feeling that he is enjoying a "wilderness experience"—a sense of being so far removed from the sights and sounds of civilization that he is alone with nature. . . .

Primitive areas should be carefully selected and should be managed for the sole and unequivocal purpose of maintaining their primitive characteristics. . . . There should be no development of public roads, permanent habitations, or recreation facilities of any sort. . . . Any economic use of the area, such as the grazing of livestock, that may exist at the time of its establishment should be discontinued as soon as practicable and equitable, and no further commercial utilization of the resources should be allowed.

Class VI—Historic and Cultural Sites: Sites of major historic or cultural significance, either local, regional, or national. . . . Examples are The Hermitage, Mount Vernon, the Civil War battle areas, the historic Indian dwellings in Mesa Verde National Park, and the Picture Rocks in Michigan. . . . The primary management objective should be to effect such restoration as may be necessary, to protect them from deterioration, and to interpret their significance to the public. . . .

Extending Present Programs

1. Each state, through a central agency, should develop a long-range plan for outdoor recreation, to provide adequate opportunities for the public, to acquire additional areas where necessary, and to preserve outstanding natural sites.

2. Local governments should give greater emphasis to the needs of their citizens for outdoor recreation by considering it in all land-use planning, opening areas with recreation potential to use, and where necessary, acquiring new areas.

3. States should seek to work out interstate arrangements where the recreation-seeking public overflows political boundaries. The Federal Government should assist in meeting these interstate demand situations.

4. Systematic and continuing research, both fundamental and applied, should be promoted to provide the basis for sound planning and decisions.

5. Immediate action should be taken by Federal, state, and local governments to reserve or acquire additional water, beach, and shoreline areas, particularly near centers of population.

6. Full provision for acquiring shoreline lands for public access and use should be made in reservoir developments.

7. Surface rights to surplus Federal lands suitable for recreation should be transferred without cost to state or local governments with reversion clauses.

8. Open-space programs for metropolitan areas should be continued.

9. Congress should enact legislation to provide for the establishment and preservation of certain primitive areas as "wilderness areas."

10. Certain rivers of unusual scientific, aesthetic, and recreation value should be allowed to remain in their free-flowing state and natural setting without man-made alterations.

11. States should use their regulatory power to zone areas for maximum recreation benefit, maintain quality, and ensure public safety in conflicts between recreation and other uses and in conflicts among recreation uses.

12. Recreation areas should be strongly defended against encroachments from nonconforming uses, both public and private. Where recreation land must be taken for another public use, it should be replaced with other land of similar quality and comparable location.

13. Public agencies should assure adequate access to water-based recreation opportunities by acquisition of access areas, easements across private lands, zoning of shorelines, consideration of water access in road design and construction, and opening of now restricted waters such as municipal reservoirs.

14. Interpretive and educational programs should be intensified and broadened to promote appreciation and understanding of natural, scientific, and historic values.

15. Outdoor recreation should be emphasized in federally constructed or licensed multipurpose water developments and thus granted full consideration in the planning, design, and construction of such projects.

16. Recreation should be recognized as a motivating purpose in programs and projects for pollution control and as a necessary objective in the allocation of funds therefor. . . . In most major cities, pollution has destroyed valuable recreation opportunities, just where they are needed most. As a sanitation measure alone, the abatement of pollution is a necessity; inherently, it is also one of the best means of increasing recreation opportunities. . . .

17. Flood-plain zoning should be used wherever possible as a method to preserve attractive reaches of rivers and streams for

public recreation in addition to the other benefits from such zoning.

18. The Federal Government and the states should recognize the potential recreation values in highway-construction programs and assure that they are developed.

19. Activities under watershed and other agricultural conservation programs should be oriented toward greater recreation benefits for the public. [After the ORRRC report was submitted in January 1962, the Watershed Protection and Flood Prevention Act was passed in late 1962. See "Small Watershed Projects," in this section, below.]

20. The states should encourage the public use of private lands by taking the lead in working out such arrangements as leases for hunting and fishing, scenic easements, and providing protection for landowners who allow the public to use their lands.

21. All levels of government must provide continuing and adequate funds for outdoor recreation. In most cases, this will require a substantial increase over present levels.

22. State and local governments should consider the use of general obligation and revenue bonds to finance land acquisition and capital improvements for outdoor recreation.

23. State and local governments should consider other financing devices such as season user fees, dedicated funds, and use of uncollected refunds of gasoline taxes paid by pleasure-boat owners.

24. States should take the lead in extending technical and financial assistance to local governments to meet outdoor recreation requirements.

25. Public agencies should adopt a system of user fees designed to recapture at least a significant portion of the operation and maintenance costs of providing outdoor recreation activities that involve the exclusive use of a facility or require special facilities.

26. In addition to outright acquisition, local governments should consider the use of such devices as easements, zoning,

cluster developments, and open-land tax policies to supplement the supply of outdoor recreation opportunities.

27. Public agencies should stimulate desirable gifts of land and money from private individuals and groups for outdoor recreation purposes. The work of private, nonprofit organizations in providing and enhancing opportunities should be encouraged.

28. Government should stimulate and encourage the provision of outdoor recreation opportunities by private enterprise.

29. Where feasible, concessioners should be encouraged to provide facilities and visitor services on Federal lands under appropriate supervision. Where this is not feasible, the Federal Government should build facilities and lease them to private business for operation.

A Bureau of Outdoor Recreation

A Bureau of Outdoor Recreation should be established in the Department of the Interior. . . .

Specifically, the new bureau would—

1. Coordinate the recreation activities of the more than twenty Federal agencies whose activities affect outdoor recreation. . . .

The Federal agencies have responded to increasing pressures for outdoor recreation. The National Park Service is at the midpoint of "Mission 66"—a ten-year program designed to make more effective use of the National Park System. "Operation Outdoors," the first step in a Forest Service plan for developing the outdoor recreation potential of the national forests, is nearing completion. The Corps of Engineers, Bureau of Reclamation, and Tennessee Valley Authority have devoted increased study and effort to developing recreation potential at public reservoirs. The Bureaus of Land Management, Sport Fisheries and Wildlife, and Reclamation—each of which administers areas serving recreation purposes —are seeking legislative authority to recognize outdoor recreation in their programs. In order for each agency to participate fully in a national recreation effort, there should be a consistent approach to similar problems of recreation development, regardless of administrative jurisdiction. . . .

2. Assist state and local governments with technical aid in planning and administration, including the development of standards for personnel, procedures, and operations.

3. Administer a grants-in-aid program to states for planning and for development and acquisition of needed areas.

4. Act as a clearinghouse for information and guide, stimulate, and sponsor research as needed.

5. Encourage interstate and regional cooperation, including Federal participation where necessary.

To assure that recreation policy and planning receive attention at a high level and to promote interdepartmental coordination, there should be established a recreation advisory council, consisting of the Secretaries of Interior, Agriculture, and Defense, with the Secretary of the Interior as chairman. Other agencies would be invited to participate on an *ad hoc* basis when matters affecting their interests are under consideration by the council.

The recreation advisory council would provide broad policy guidance on all matters affecting outdoor recreation activities and programs carried out by the Bureau of Outdoor Recreation. The Secretary of the Interior should be required to seek such guidance in the administration of the bureau.

Initially the new bureau should be staffed where possible by transfer of experienced personnel from existing Federal agencies. It should have regional offices.

A research advisory committee consisting of professional people from government, academic life, and private business should be established to advise the bureau on its research activities.

It is urged that each state designate a focal point within its governmental structure to work with the bureau. This focal point, perhaps one of the existing state agencies, could also serve to coordinate state recreation planning and activities and be responsible for a comprehensive state outdoor recreation plan.

A Grants-in-Aid Program

A Federal grants-in-aid program should be established to stimulate and assist the states in meeting the demand for outdoor recreation. This program, administered by the proposed Bureau of Outdoor Recreation, would promote state planning and acquisition and development of areas to meet the demands of the public. [For a summary of the ORRRC recommendations that have been effected, see Editor's Introduction to this section.]

CONSERVATION OF MAN AND HIS ENVIRONMENT [2]

Science and technology hold the keys to the kingdom of abundance—and planning, long a favorite whipping-boy of "practical" men, is now the one indispensable science. . . . We have the insight and the power to conserve, and the existence of what I will call areas of quiet crisis in resource management indicts us, separately and collectively, for failure to act. . . . We have conquered outer and neglected the "inner" space that is our home. . . . The level of military preparedness required by the cold war has necessarily made our total performance lopsided. . . .

The irony of our situation is that the quiet crisis in conservation of the sixties arises, in part, from our very success as a nation. As science opens up new avenues of abundance, it also opens up new opportunities for careless exploitation—and the classic pattern of the past repeats itself. The modern land raiders, like their predecessors, insist always that the present is paramount and assert their right to misuse the land. The operator of a manufacturing plant that befouls the air, or the owner of a pulp mill that corrupts a river, who asks the insolent question, "Which is more important, payrolls or picnics?" is really saying something like this: "The public be damned! Let the government, or those who live downwind or downstream, undo the damage I have caused." Such materialistic thinking dismisses environment preservation as "mere aesthetics"; the truth is that the so-called

[2] From *The Conservation Challenge of the Sixties,* the Horace M. Albright Lecture, delivered by Stewart L. Udall, Secretary of the Interior, before the School of Forestry, University of California, Berkeley, April 19, 1963. Text from *Planning and Civic Comment.* 29:1-4+. D. '63; 30:1-4+. Mr. '64.

amenities are now necessities, and the so-called intangibles are tangible indeed!

This is also the implicit philosophy of the subdivider who bulldozes a streamside woodland, the billboard advertiser who blocks the highway with eyesores, the municipalities that dump sewage into bays and riverways. It should be perfectly clear that no one has a "right" to pollute the air or water or despoil the last remaining areas of green countryside around our cities—any more than the nineteenth century resource raiders had a right to destroy the forests or the soil. . . .

The answer, of course, lies in a new land ethic and new forms of social control. We can have clean air, clean rivers and a green countryside if we decide that our environment should have parity with payrolls and profits. Once, by law, we make pollution abatement part of the cost of doing business, men in laboratories will quickly devise machines and gadgets to control the things that cause contamination.

But the erosion of our environment will continue unless we make public rights paramount—which means that we put the future first. The conservation of man, through conservation of his environment, must become a major national objective. . . .

Clearly, the task of wise resource management is now a joint venture between government, universities, and the managers of industry. Much of our success in conservation during this generation has resulted from the increasing commitment of American business to conservation research and conservation practices. By their very nature, however, governments must plan for the long haul and concentrate on long-term projects, but enlightened men of business have also learned that it is good business to look to the horizon. . . .

The greatest water problem throughout the nation is the senseless and extravagant waste that results from the pollution of our rivers and streams by the sewage of cities and industries—a practice as blind and destructive as that which led to the leveling of our finest forests. A pollution-control program is getting underway, but most of our rivers are a national disgrace and our water awakening is still in the future. . . .

The quiet crisis in conservation in our country is most acute when we consider our outdoor environment. . . . Our fascination with the dazzling things of an inventive era has seemingly diminished our love for the land. This trend has, of course, been quickened by the emphasis on urbanization and mobility, the seductions of spectatorship, the requirements of industrial growth, and the air-conditioned advantages that have made glassed-in living so appealing. It is understandable that, in hectic times, a sedentary and city-bound people would witness the erosion of outdoor resources without alarm.

Let us not mistake it. The deterioration of our environment has been the paramount conservation failure of the postwar years. . . . The American earth is fast losing its spaciousness and freshness and green splendor. . . . We have finally moved from a condition of land surplus to one of land shortage, and our national policy has now come full circle: east of the Mississippi, where nearly all public lands were sold off in haste, the improvidence of a policy of unlimited disposal is apparent on every hand. Choice lands that were virtually given away must now be purchased at near-prohibitive prices and returned to public ownership to fulfill the demand for outdoor recreation. Scenic tracts, such as Cape Cod and Fire Island, which were available at modest cost only a few years ago, are today almost beyond the reach of the public purse. [Cape Cod and Fire Island became National Seashores by act of Congress in 1961 and 1964, respectively.—Ed.]

The outdoor problem has been studied with thoroughness and vision. The 1962 report of the Outdoor Recreation Resources Review Commission contains a comprehensive set of findings and guidelines. Do we have the will to implement this report? . . .

If large areas are to be preserved it is no exaggeration to say that what this generation saves is all that will be saved. . . .

RECREATION IN THE GREAT SOCIETY [3]

The 88th Congress has passed more than thirty important conservation bills. [Many of these measures resulted from recom-

[3] From prepared presidential campaign statement of President Lyndon B. Johnson, Portland, Oregon, September 17, 1964. mimeo. Office of the White House Press Secretary. 1600 Pennsylvania Ave, N.W. Washington, D.C. 20501. '64.

mendations of the Outdoor Recreation Resources Review Commission. See "Outdoor Recreation for America," above.] A new land and water conservation fund will help states and cities set aside spots of beauty for recreation and pleasure. A Wilderness Act will guarantee all Americans the natural magnificence which has been . . . [their] heritage. Water research and water planning bills will speed development for the soaring water needs of a growing nation. We established continental America's first new national park in seventeen years, twenty-three new national park areas, . . . four new national seashores, and a national riverway. We began a new Bureau of Outdoor Recreation so that our children will have a place to hunt and fish and glory in nature. We began construction of over two hundred water resources projects with about seventy more scheduled for 1965. . . . [See "Small Watershed Projects," in this section, below.]

When America began there seemed no limit to the riches of the earth. Then came a time of reckless exploitation and ruthless plunder. Greed and ignorance combined to lay waste our resources and threaten our domain with destruction. . . .

Three changing forces are bringing a new era to conservation.

The first is growing population. By the year 2000, more than 300 million Americans will need ten times the power and two and one half times the water we now consume. Increasing pressure will take our resources and increasing leisure will tax our recreation.

The second is the triumph of technology. The bright success of science also has a darker side. The poisons and chemicals, the junked automobiles and the waste products of progress, may be one of the deadliest threats to the destruction of nature we have ever known.

The third is urbanization. More of our people are crowding into cities and cutting themselves off from nature. Access to beauty is denied and ancient values are destroyed. Conservation must move from nature's wilderness to the man-made wilderness of our cities.

All of this requires a new conservation. In the development of a new conservation I intend to press ahead on . . . [several] fronts. First, we seek to guarantee our children a place to walk and play and commune with nature. The demand on our recreational facilities is doubling each decade. We must act boldly or our future will be barren. We will move vigorously under our . . . [new] laws to acquire and develop new areas for recreation— emphasizing areas of concentrated population. And we will be ready to expand our programs to meet developing needs. A national program of scenic parkways and riverways is on the horizon. I hope to make the Potomac a conservation model for our metropolitan areas. In our cities open space must be reserved where possible, and created where preservation comes too late.

Second, we must control the waste products of technology. The air we breathe, the water we drink, our soil and our wildlife are being blighted by the chemicals and the inevitable waste products of modern life. The skeletons of discarded cars litter our countryside. Technology and production must go forward. But the same society which receives the rewards of technology must, as a cooperating whole, take responsibility for control. I intend to work with local government and industry to develop a national policy for control and disposal of technological and industrial waste. And I will work with them to carry out this policy. . . .

Third, we must increase mastery over our environment through the marvels of new technology. . . . We will cooperate with government at every level to develop all the resources while preserving all the scenic promise of an entire region. The scale of our programs must match the scope of our problems. . . .

Fourth, we must prevent urbanization and growth from ravishing the land. At this moment a working group is studying ways to protect the integrity of nature in cities and suburbs. The nation is growing. We want that growth to be a blessing and not a blight. I will suggest—in cooperation with local government and private industry—policies to help ensure that suburban building, highway construction, and industrial spread are conducted with reverence and regard for the values of nature. . . .

We must not only protect from destruction but restore what has been destroyed—not only develop old resources but create new ones—not only save the countryside but salvage the cities. It is not just the classic conservation of protection and development, but a creative conservation of restoration and innovation. Its concern is not with nature alone, but with the total relation between man and the world around him. Its object is not just man's welfare but the dignity of his spirit.

Above all, we must maintain the chance for contact with beauty. When that chance dies a light dies in all of us. Thoreau said: "A town is saved not more by the righteous men in it than by the woods . . . that surround it." And Emerson taught: "There is no police so effective as a good hill and wide pasture." We are the creation of our environment. If it becomes filthy and sordid, then the dignity of the spirit and the deepest of our values are in danger.

And once nature is destroyed or beauty blighted, it can rarely be restored. It is gone forever. It is our children who will bear the burden of our neglect. We owe it to them to keep that from happening.

ECONOMIC BENEFITS OF OUTDOOR RECREATION [4]

Outdoor recreation produces many benefits. It provides the healthful exercise necessary for individual physical fitness. It promotes mental health. It offers spiritual values, for being in the outdoors can be a deeply moving experience. It is valuable for education in the world of nature. . . . But there are also important economic effects in the provision of outdoor recreation. . . .

[4] From *Outdoor Recreation for America; a Report to the President and to the Congress by the Outdoor Recreation Resources Review Commission.* United States. Outdoor Recreation Resources Review Commission. Supt. of Docs. Washington, D.C. 20402. '62. p 75-80.

Value to the Community

Providing open space for recreation usually brings about valuable economic consequences in addition to the social benefits.

The effect of parks on adjoining land values is one example. City after city cites the experience—parks enhance the value of surrounding property. There is no over-all study of this effect, but all reports tend to support it. Minneapolis, noted for its fine park system, says that the increased values in the city due to park developments have amounted to several times the cost of the entire system. Essex County, New Jersey, found that land adjacent to parks increased in value three times as fast as other property. . . .

The use most often competing for potential park land or open space is residential development, and governments often lose money on such development—that is, it costs more to provide schools, streets, and other services than is returned in new taxes. Thus, in many instances, placing the land in recreation use may prevent a drain on the community's finances while engendering a long-term rise in surrounding property values. . . .

Effects on an Underdeveloped Area

The effects of outdoor recreation are most striking when large-scale expenditures come to a relatively underdeveloped area. An example followed completion of seven large reservoirs constructed by the Corps of Engineers in the Arkansas-White-Red River Basins in the states of Arkansas, Oklahoma, Texas, and Missouri. [Since World War II reservoirs have been used increasingly for recreation, as well as for supplying water, preventing floods, and other purposes.—Ed.]

Three of these reservoirs have been established for fifteen years, three for the past eight years, and one was opened in 1960. With one or two exceptions, the reservoirs were located in counties that had previously been underdeveloped.

All seventeen counties in the four states with significant shorelines on these reservoirs were studied, and comparisons were then made with eight adjacent counties that did not have shore-line on these reservoirs. Population growth, per capita income, annual wages, retail sales, bank deposits, taxes, and investment were considered.

In the ten-year period ending in 1960, all counties in the study lost population, but the seventeen reservoir counties lost only 8.5 per cent in contrast with the 25.1 per cent loss in the nonreservoir counties. From 1949 to 1959, annual per capita income of the reservoir counties in Arkansas increased from $669 to $1,053, or 57 per cent, in contrast to an increase of $349 to $431, or only 23 per cent, in the nonreservoir counties.

The gain in bank deposits also favored reservoir counties:

	1949	1958
17 reservoir counties	$82.6 million	$130.0 million
8 nonreservoir counties	15.1 million	21.2 million

The growth of local tax collections points up the value of business generated by reservoir recreation. From 1945 to 1956, ten Oklahoma reservoir county tax levies increased nearly 64 per cent. Two selected Oklahoma nonreservoir county collections were up only 3.8 per cent for the same period. In that period, school taxes were up 296 per cent in the reservoir counties compared with 190 per cent in the nonreservoir counties.

Another aspect of the effect of reservoir recreation has been the steady annual increase of investment in overnight accommodations from an initial investment in 1945 of $1.4 million to the 1959 total of $20.8 million in the fourteen reservoir counties for which data are available. These capital expenditures are, of course, in addition to income generated by visiting recreation seekers.

Still another element of capital investment has been the increasing annual expenditure on private homes and cabins near the reservoirs. This type of investment, in the fourteen counties for which data are available, has grown from $86,000 in 1945 to $25.7 million by 1959. The current average expenditure in this form of investment is about $3.2 million annually.

While all the economic gains in the reservoir counties may not be directly attributable to the new lakes, it is undoubtedly true that outdoor recreation has had a dramatic beneficial effect. Almost every economic sign indicates that the reservoir counties are better off. Indeed, in some, it has almost changed the entire way of life, as the stimulus offered by the recreation dollars has had far-reaching ramifications. New schools and better public services have, in turn, brightened other economic prospects.

These cases are special in that large-scale recreation expenditures came to a comparatively depressed area in a rather short period, but they do illustrate the power of the recreation dollar.

A Major Market

In addition to effects on local economies, outdoor recreation plays an important part in the economic life of the country. The millions and millions of Americans seeking the outdoors are generating a huge demand for goods and services. Satisfying this demand is a big business, and it is getting bigger. . . .

Tourist expenditures have been estimated at about $25 billion annually. In 1957, tourists were estimated to be spending at least a billion dollars a year visiting each of the states of New York, Florida, New Jersey, and Pennsylvania. Six other states reaped at least half a billion each from visitors—Illinois, Michigan, Virginia, Kentucky, Texas, and California.

In 1959, the total estimated dollar value of purchases of major sporting goods was just under $2 billion. Of this, approximately $1.5 billion was for items related to outdoor recreation.

An estimated $2.1 billion was spent at the retail level during 1958 for boats, engines, accessories, safety equipment, fuel, insurance, docking, maintenance, launching, storage, repair, and boat club membership.

Fishermen are reported to spend $3 billion annually on their sport.

Direct expenditures by government for providing outdoor recreation were over a billion dollars in 1960. Federal and state agencies spent $380 million, and the remainder was supplied by local government.

It has been estimated that visitors to Federal and state parks, forests, and reservoirs spend over $11 billion annually. This does not include expenditures of the large portion of the population that seeks its recreation on private lands. . . .

On the basis of these indicators and from general consideration of the field, consumer spending for outdoor recreation is now estimated to be in the neighborhood of $20 billion annually. Aside from a small fraction for licenses and privilege fees, the bulk of recreation expenditures go for food, lodging, transportation, boats, and other equipment. Thus, the principal recipients of these expenditures are automotive and equipment dealers, boat dealers, purveyors of food and lodging, sporting-goods dealers, and service-station owners. These expenditures are made in three general zones—in the home community, en route, and at the recreation area. Roughly one third of the total expenditure is made in each zone.

The great importance of location is clear for retailers who seek to obtain a share of the "en route" and "at or near recreation area" expenditures. This explains to a considerable degree the shift in real estate values along major recreation access routes and in the immediate neighborhood of newly established recreation areas.

Thus, expenditures of recreation seekers provide a significant element in the economic life of the community. An extreme example of this effect is afforded by Teton County, Wyoming, which contains the Grand Teton National Park and is adjacent to Yellowstone National Park. In 1958, tourist expenditures of nearly $7 million produced a business of over $12 million, or about 71 per cent of the total business generated in the county by all economic activity.

In 1956, some 2.5 million persons visited the Great Smoky Mountains National Park in southeastern Tennessee and southwestern North Carolina and spent about $28 million within an area extending 30 miles beyond the park boundaries. In 1958, nearly 3.2 million persons spent an estimated $35 million in the same area.

But this is not all. For as the volume of recreation expands, it may bring about additional capital investment, which enlarges the scope of the community's economic activities. The desire of recreation seekers for a summer cabin or a second home near a lake or seashore or in the mountains induces long-term capital investment, as distinct from direct retail purchases. For instance, the estimated 28,000 summer homes in New Hampshire provide a market for real estate, building and other materials, and labor. The summer residents of these homes increase the population by one fifth—bringing that many more customers to local businesses. In the state of Maine, recreation property values represent 10 per cent of the total real property valuation of the state, and of this total over 64 per cent was accounted for by privately owned recreation residences.

Thus, while recreation is and should be considered one of that order of services which must be provided for its benefit to the public without a dollar-and-cents accounting of immediate benefits, it does make sound fiscal sense. In urban areas, recreation is often a wise economic use of land, increasing values beyond its cost; in some underdeveloped areas, it may be a means of economic rebirth; and throughout the nation it provides a major market for goods and services.

SMALL WATERSHED PROJECTS [5]

Forty-four per cent of the population prefers water-based recreation activities over any other, and this trend is on the increase.

How will the demand for more water-based public recreation areas be met? Many state and local governments are finding a solution through the United States Department of Agriculture's Small Watershed Program, which has been so successful in flood

[5] From article by Hollis R. Williams, deputy administrator for watersheds, Soil Conservation Service, United States Department of Agriculture. *Recreation.* 57:276-8. Je. '64. Reprinted by permission.

prevention, erosion control, agricultural water management, and supplying water for municipal and industrial uses, and fish and wildlife development.

It has been evident for some time that small watershed projects offer excellent opportunities for public recreation developments. The ORRRC [Outdoor Recreation Resources Review Commission] report [see "Outdoor Recreation for America," in this section, above] states that "the broad scope of the small watershed program places it in a particularly favorable position to contribute to public recreation opportunities. Most of the nation's small watersheds, including many adjacent to metropolitan areas, are eligible for treatment."

The potential contribution of small watershed projects in meeting the public recreation needs was recognized by Congress when it passed legislation to broaden the Watershed Protection and Flood Prevention Act (Public Law 566) late in 1962. Now the Federal Government through the Soil Conservation Service, may cost share up to 50 per cent for enlarging dams for recreation use, acquiring land, easements, and rights-of-way for the larger reservoir and adjacent land, and in construction of minimum basic facilities needed for public health, safety, and access.

There are, of course, certain general policies and provisions surrounding the use of this new recreation authorization. For one thing, the recreation development must be available to the public. There must be at least one access road, and the entire immediate shoreline of a reservoir must be open to the public, thus preventing private landowners from exclusive use of any section of the shoreline. Local sponsors may charge a user fee to cover maintenance and operating costs.

Watershed projects under Public Law 566 are local projects. They are initiated, partly financed, built, and maintained by the local sponsoring groups. The sponsors also own all the structures that might be built. Groups eligible to sponsor or co-sponsor a watershed project include soil and water conservation districts, municipalities, counties, conservancy districts, state agencies, and others so authorized by the state government. Applications ap-

proved by the designated state agency and the SCS state conservationist are sent to the Washington SCS office for further
action.

The new recreation provision of the Small Watershed Program has already been widely accepted, particularly by state
park and fish and wildlife agencies, county governments, and
municipalities. The recreation lakes, their operation, and maintenance remain under control of local organizations or state
agencies and can be operated as a part of the state park systems
or in whatever manner local organizations may determine as
consistent with state policies.

Watershed projects have repeatedly proven their worth
through the nation in preventing destructive floods, halting soil
erosion, supplying water for municipal and industrial needs, enhancing fish and wildlife resources, providing water for irriga-
tion, and improving drainage. The flood-detention reservoirs, designed to catch peak runoff water from rainfall, are ideally suited
for recreation and for fish and wildlife developments. Water im-
poundments backed by the earthen dams range in size from less
than ten acres to more than two hundred acres. The average
runs about thirty acres. To date, there have been more than
three thousand such reservoirs constructed in watershed projects.

Prior to the new provision, many of these reservoirs were developed for recreation purposes through the generosity of individual landowners who controlled the land surrounding them.
These developments, however, have been minimal except where
state and local governments were involved in the undertaking.

Such an undertaking is well illustrated in Kentucky's Mud
River multipurpose watershed project, where the State Department of Fish and Wildlife Resources has sponsored the recreation phase of the project to serve the needs of an estimated half
million visitors annually. One of the project's twenty-six flood-
detention reservoirs was enlarged to create a nine-hundred-acre
lake in picturesque rolling, wooded country. The lake will be
used for swimming, fishing, boating, and water skiing. The state
purchased adjoining land for a public park for picnicking, hik-

ing, and camping. Thirty miles of roads have been constructed, and electricity and telephone lines have been installed to service the area.

It is expected that tourists, attracted by the new lake and recreation facilities, will add greatly to the local economy which has depended primarily on agriculture up to now. [See "Economic Benefits of Outdoor Recreation" in this section, above.] The new lake is the only body of water of any size within a hundred miles.

Recreation is not the only way local people will benefit from the project. It also offers flood protection to the 1,860 farmers in the 240,000-acre watershed. One community has tapped one of the watershed project's reservoirs for much needed municipal water. As a result, small industries have sprung up and others have expanded.

The city of Plain Dealing, Louisiana, sponsored the recreation development in the Upper West Fork Cypress Bayou Watershed project. The city now has two lakes, one with 104 and the other with 98 surface acres, for recreation. The larger reservoir also furnishes the community with 750,000 gallons of water daily for municipal use. A sixty-acre park adjoins the lake and has been developed for recreation by community, civic, and service groups, businessmen, and individuals.

The lakes were stocked with fish by the Louisiana Fish and Wildlife Service. As many as three thousand people have been attracted to the lakes in a single day. It is interesting to note that when small watershed projects now being developed in Louisiana are completed, they will add more than thirty-five hundred surface acres of water in the state. Most of this area will be developed for some recreation uses.

In 1963, the first year the recreation provision of the watershed act was made available, a total of sixty-one proposals were made to add recreation in fifty-five watershed projects in twenty-nine states. The cost of these developments—to enlarge structures, obtain land rights, and install minimum basic facilities—would run approximately $27.4 million, of which local groups would be responsible for $14.8 million and the Federal Government allotting $12.6 million. The developments would provide for an estimated 3.7 million user-days of water-based recreation annually.

The Department of Agriculture also encourages church and private organizations, such as sportsmen's clubs, youth groups, and the like in developing recreation sites in watershed projects. Since these developments are not open to the general public, there is no cost sharing, but technical help and loans are available. Private groups have been quick to recognize the recreation potential of watershed lakes. For example, the Tennessee-Arkansas-Mississippi Council of Girl Scouts is sponsoring the recreation development around one of the reservoirs in Tennessee's Porters Creek Watershed project as a permanent summer camping area for the council's nine thousand scouts.

The council owned twelve hundred acres on which a watershed flood-detention dam was to be built. The council granted an easement to build the dam on its property and paid $56,000 to enlarge it for recreation purposes. How was it financed? Virginia Jones, the council's executive director, said, "We don't figure in *dollars*. We figure in *cookies*. The lake has cost us about 300,000 boxes of cookies, dutifully sold by Girl Scouts in the three states."

When completed, the camp will house more than five hundred girls and their counselors at one time. Girl Scouts have also developed a summer camp in Georgia's Sautee River Watershed project and have a $250,000 development under way in the Wildlife Creek Watershed project in Oklahoma.

As of February 1 [1964], 2,056 applications had been made for watershed development under Public Law 566. Of this number, 530 are under construction and an additional 618 are in the planning stage. There are 13,000 watersheds under 250,000 acres in the United States, of which slightly more than 8,000 need project action . . . for flood prevention, erosion control, and the like. The USDA believes recreation developments could be incorporated in several thousands of these projects.

Although the United States is endowed with many natural water acres, there are many factors limiting them for recreation development such as lack of public access, pollution, and geographic location. Small watershed projects, on the other hand, can be and are being sponsored in almost any part of the nation. Developed projects have brought water-based recreation closer to hundreds of thousands of people already. In the future, small watershed projects can do much in filling the outdoor recreation demands of millions.

THE NATIONAL PARKS [6]

When we speak of "the national parks" of the United States, our first thought, naturally, is of the . . . [thirty-two] areas strictly so designated by Congress, most of them places of transcendent beauty and of natural marvels; such parks as Grand Canyon, Yellowstone, Crater Lake, and Yosemite. Actually in the National Park System there are . . . [over 200], and every one of them may justly be called a national park, even though some are classified as "monuments," others as "historic sites," some as "military parks" and others even as "parkways" ["seashores," "riverways," and "recreation areas"]. The naming is several, but the purpose and effect is that of a full representation of the American story— of the earth we live upon, of the races who lived here before the white man came, of the great struggle for possession of the continent, of the winning of the republic, and finally of our own political and social life. . . . Each [park] has been set aside for preservation, to minister both to the physical and to the spiritual needs of all Americans living and yet unborn.

There has never in the history of nations been a cultural achievement like this one. . . . We have preserved a part of our precious heritage before it became too little and too late. . . .

It is a curious fact that the first, and still one of the world's greatest national parks—Yellowstone—was in a very real sense a

[6] From *The Fifth Essence: An Invitation to Share in Our Eternal Heritage*, by Freeman Tilden, short-story writer, novelist, consultant to the National Park Service. United States. National Park Trust Fund Board. Washington, D.C. 20240. '57.

gift by individuals to the people of the United States. True, it was public domain in 1870, when the [N.P.] Langford party, with a soldier escort, journeyed into a wilderness of which strange tales had been told, stories of nature's prodigies that were commonly scouted as monumental mendacity. They came, they saw, they marveled; and then, being human, the greed came upon them to possess, by filing claims, this potentially profitable region. . . . [But] gathered around a campfire one night, in the presence of so much beauty and wonder, they resolutely decided that this wilderness should not belong to any man, but to all men. . . .

They were not the first men who spoke of "national parks" . . . but these men *did something* about it. They put aside their personal interests and joined in an effort to create a park. Less than two years later, President Grant signed an act establishing Yellowstone National Park as "a public park or pleasuring ground." A "pleasuring ground"! It has been that indeed, and in ways that could not have suggested themselves so clearly in the seventies of the last century. Is it, in view of all this, too much to say that Yellowstone came to the people as a donation? . . .

With the exception of thrilling Yosemite, which passed from state authority into the national cluster, one park after another was added to Yellowstone, mostly from Federal lands. Hot Springs in Arkansas, a Federal "reserve" since 1832, became a park in 1921. Big Bend National Park in Texas was the gift of the people of Texas to the nation. But for the most part the succession of parks represented a transfer, and a new conception of land management, of the public domain. . . .

By 1916 it had become obvious that the system of parks had grown to the point where a special government agency was needed to administer it. As a bureau in the Department of the Interior, the National Park Service was created. None too soon; for the scope of the trusteeship was enormously enlarged in 1933 by the transfer of national monuments and national military parks from the War Department, and of many monuments from the Forest Service of the Department of Agriculture, and later by the creation of historic sites in the fields of history and archaeology.

The words of the act which established the National Park Service should be known to every American. . . . It imposed upon an agency of the government the obligation to see that the American people should have preserved for them the precious evidences of the national greatness—not merely of its heroes and actions, but of the very land itself: ". . . to conserve the scenery, the natural and historic objects and the wildlife . . . to provide for enjoyment of the same in such manner and by such means as will leave them unimpaired for the enjoyment of future generations." . . .

From the director down, the Park Service employees are career men. It must be so. The peculiar nature of the work—a strange combination of policemanship, tactful public relations, instruction, entertainment, and self-discipline—necessarily appeals only to a certain type of man.

The "father" of the National Park System [was] Stephen T. Mather, that Chicago industrialist who made a fortune out of Twenty Mule Team Borax and found expression for his idealism and love of nature by being the first director of the service. . . . He gave himself, and he gave his money. In his case, *himself* was the more important. Yet when the toll road through Tioga Pass across Yosemite Park stood in the way of public use of the Park, he and his friends bought it for the people; when the Giant Forest in Sequoia Park had to be saved, he found the purses, including his own, to do it.

Vital to any administrative program that envisages the fullest and finest use of the national parks—whether areas of solacing wilderness or historic shrines—is the work of creating understanding. It is true that each preserved monument "speaks for itself." But unfortunately it speaks partly in a language that the average visitor cannot comprehend. Beauty and the majesty of natural forces need no interlocutor. They constitute a personal spiritual experience. But when the question is "why?" or "what?" or "how did this come to be?" your Park Service people must have the answers. . . .

The naturalist must know, and accurately; the historian at Yorktown battlefield must be able to project a faithful drama.

And it is the digging of the archaeologists, at Mesa Verde and the other prehistoric monuments, that has made it possible for the modern visitor to feel that these ruins are a part of the ever-living American story. . . .

Then there are the museums, both of the nature areas and of the historical. . . . The National Park Service, having a specialist who has attained an international reputation in his field, has been working for years toward the ideal in museum exhibits. How far it has gone in this quest of making the on-the-spot museum a simple, easily understood but dynamic factor in area-interpretation will be readily seen in a visit to such a battlefield park as Manassas (Bull Run); to such a prehistoric Indian monument as Ocmulgee; or to the Federal Hall Memorial in Wall Street, New York City, . . . Here, on the site where George Washington was first inaugurated, you will see, by means of lifelike dioramas and skillfully selected period material, the story of the colonial printer [John Peter Zenger] whose stubborn resistance helped so greatly to bring freedom of the press, as well as a larger freedom to America.

WHAT THE STATES ARE DOING [7]

In accordance with the United States Constitution, all powers not delegated to the nation reside in the states, and it is thus a state responsibility to authorize the establishment of local services. Moreover, state agencies render statewide services that are beyond the scope of the subdivisions of the state. . . .

The legal authority for the operation of public programs, by schools, parks, or separate recreation agencies, is granted to the local communities by the states. Each state designates through its own enabling laws the means by which counties and municipalities may operate recreation programs. The legislation may indicate the administrative structure, the functions to be per-

[7] From *Recreation in American Life*, by Reynold E. Carlson, Theodore R. Deppe, and Janet R. MacLean. © 1963. By Wadsworth Publishing Company, Inc., Belmont, California. Reprinted by permission of the publisher. p 251-69. (Reynold E. Carlson is professor of recreation; Theodore R. Deppe and Janet R. MacLean are associate professors of recreation—all at Indiana University.)

formed, the methods of financing, tax limitations, and the like. Thus the states perform the essential service of providing a base upon which local communities may build.

Services to Local Units of Government

In such fields as education, health, and welfare, the state renders direct services to communities through separate state offices and staffs. In only a few instances have the states given comparable services in the field of recreation; but where they have done so, local recreation programs have shown improvement both in numbers and in quality. . . .

Where special recreation agencies do not exist, recreation advisory services to local units of government are frequently rendered by departments of education, or agencies concerned with health, welfare, planning, parks, forests, and conservation. Colleges and universities and extension services of the colleges of agriculture may also give such services. Inter-agency committees have been organized in some states for this purpose.

State services to local communities include: studying recreation needs and programs and making recommendations for meeting needs through the expansion of present services or the establishment of new ones; providing information to local communities on methods of financing, administering, and conducting community programs; helping local communities enrich and improve recreation opportunities; acting as a means of exchange of information and ideas among local communities to effect improvements in programs and services; assisting in the recruitment and selection of personnel; conducting training courses and workshops for recreation leaders; and developing standards for the conduct of programs. Some states give financial assistance as well as advisory services for the development of local recreation programs.

All of the states own land, with about three fourths of the state-owned land lying in the seventeen western states. States with large holdings usually have parks, forests, wildlife reserves, and income-producing lands, which they lease to private users for grazing, mining, and oil producing. Other states have only small parks and lands on which state-owned buildings are placed.

States not only hold land specifically for recreation but in addition hold vast acreages that, although acquired primarily for economic purposes, are increasingly receiving recreation use. It may be said that the major service of states in recreation, apart from granting authority to local units to operate programs, is the provision of outdoor areas.

States hold title to about 80 million acres of land, about 50 million of which are grazing lands held for income purposes, primarily for schools. State lands upon which outdoor recreation is a recognized use totaled 36.6 million acres in 1960. . . .

So remunerative have businesses catering to travelers and vacationers become that some states make concerted efforts to attract tourists. State agencies engage in advertising; preparing and distributing booklets, maps, and folders; and maintaining information centers for the convenience of tourists. . . . Private associations, such as state chambers of commerce, also participate in such promotion programs.

There are certain special groups to which the states offer recreation services. Among them are state-maintained institutions such as hospitals, correctional institutions, and homes for the orphaned or the aged. Mental-health institutions particularly recognize the values of recreation and sponsor therapeutic recreation programs. Another service to a special group is that provided through state agricultural extension services. Rural residents, both adults and children, benefit from these programs. The state cooperates with the county agricultural agent and the home demonstration agents at the local level.

Regulations affecting recreation are of two types: those protecting the users and those protecting the resources. The state assumes the responsibility for regulating activities that might be harmful to the health, safety, and morals of its citizens. Certain types of commercial amusements, such as gambling, are regulated or prohibited, as are other activities in which there is potential danger to children or adults. Organized camps, fishing lodges, and resorts are regulated and inspected to safeguard the health and safety of their patrons. Swimming pools are required to maintain certain standards of cleanliness. State laws protecting natural resources include those controlling hunting and fishing, protecting land from fire and vandalism, preventing water pollution, and preserving plant life. . . .

State Recreation Commissions or Boards

Many leaders in the field of recreation believe that only through recognition of recreation as a separate function of state government, along with health, welfare, and education, can recreation services contribute in the fullest extent to the well-being of the citizens of the state. In spite of this point of view, few states have established separate commissions or boards.

The state commissions and boards do not operate recreation programs themselves. Their functions are to advise local communities, sponsor training institutes, organize conferences, and make surveys. North Carolina, which established a State Recreation Commission in 1945, was the first state to have a separate recreation agency. Vermont was second in 1947, when its State Recreation Board was established. California followed, also in 1947, with a Recreation Commission; its functions were later transferred to the Department of Natural Resources.

Washington and Colorado created state park and recreation commissions. Some other states have recreation consultants, responsible either to an established agency or directly to the governor. . . .

State Parks

State parks in their inception were set aside as historic shrines or places of outstanding natural beauty, somewhat intermediary between municipal parks and national parks. Some parks were intended to protect typical scenery so that future generations might know what the land was like before the coming of the white man. As time passed, there were included within the state park systems certain areas with a different emphasis, in which the land itself was subordinate to the recreational usage. These were places devoted for the most part to active recreation pursuits —swimming beaches, boating waters, campgrounds, winter sports areas, or, in some cases, playfields similar to those in city parks.

There is a difference of opinion among state park leaders as to the extent to which state parks should provide for active recreation. In many parks, swimming, horseback riding, camping, fishing, canoeing, boating, and hiking are accepted as appropriate activities, although the understanding and appreciation of natural and historic features are still regarded as the chief reason for state parks. In coming years, state park agencies may find it necessary to provide for more of the active recreation pursuits.

Provisions for Visitors

Hotels, inns, vacation cabins, campgrounds, concession stands, picnic shelters, and amphitheaters are usually provided for the comfort and convenience of the visiting public. Swimming pools and beaches with lifeguards are commonly found. In some parks, personnel to conduct recreation activities are employed.

Because many park administrators are convinced that the fullest and wisest enjoyment of parks depends upon understanding them, interpretive services have been instituted in some places. Naturalists or historians conduct field trips, give lectures, arrange displays, conduct evening campfire programs with slides and films, and prepare publications. In many cases there are trailside museums, small zoos, nature trails, and trailside displays to inform the visitors. Historic parks often include buildings, burial grounds, or sites of important events around which the parks' interpretive programs center.

Background of State Parks

The first state park in the United States was the Yosemite Grant, created in California in 1864 from land committed to the state by Congress. The concept of reserving superlative natural areas for public use was a new one. This grant, comprising a spectacular glacier-cut valley and the nearby Mariposa Grove of Big Trees, was a forerunner of our vast systems of national and state parks. It was transferred to the National Park System in 1890. The second state park, established by Michigan at Mackinac Island in 1885, was especially interesting because of its historic backgrounds, having served French, English, and Americans in the dramatic days of the fur trade. A small piece of property was set aside by the state of New York at Niagara Falls in 1885. The first parks were administered individually; state park systems were a much later development.

Following these beginnings, a number of other states moved to establish parks. The movement lagged, however, until the 1920's. In 1921, Stephen T. Mather, dynamic first director of the National Park Service, brought together in Des Moines, Iowa, a group of people interested in furthering the development of state parks. As a result of this meeting, the National Conference on State Parks, which has devoted itself ever since to state park improvement, was organized.

It remained for the depression years of the 1930's to bring to fruition the development of state parks. A number of states, particularly in the southern United States, trace their park program to these years. The National Park Service was given the responsibility of working with the states to develop parks. From 1928 to 1941 the parks grew from 484 areas and 2.7 million acres of land to 1,335 areas and 4.2 million acres of land. Many camps, lodges, picnic areas, roads, trails, shelter houses, and the like, on state park land also had their inception as a part of the public works program of the depression years. Reduction of travel during World War II caused a decline in state park programs, maintenance, and attendance. Expansion came to a virtual standstill.

Expansion in State Parks

After World War II, attendance increased sharply, from 92.5 million in 1946 to 259 million in 1960. Land acreage did not increase proportionately to attendance during this period. There were 4.6 million acres in 1946 as compared with 5.6 million in 1960. The numbers of areas increased somewhat more rapidly, from 1,531 in 1946 to 2,664 in 1960.

The most startling increase in state park usage has come in camping. State parks in the South and parts of the East, which campers once used only slightly, have been overwhelmed with demands for campsites. Provisions for campers increased markedly in state parks between 1955 and 1960 alone, yet not as fast as the numbers of campers. During this period there was a 60 per cent increase in the number of individual campsites, while the number of tent and trailer "camper days" increased from 7.6 million in 1955 to 16.2 million in 1960. The numbers of hotels, lodges, cabins, group camps, restaurants, and refreshment stands likewise increased, but at a much slower rate.

The use of state parks has expanded about five times as fast as the population since World War II. Several states have made strenuous efforts to meet demands and to prepare for anticipated growth. In 1960, New York authorized a $75 million bond issue for the development of 25,000 additional acres of state park and recreation land. California embarked in 1956 on an enormous program of acquisition and development, particularly of ocean shore properties. The program was financed by royalties from state-owned oil lands.

States differ greatly in the way in which they secure land and finance the development of state parks. Much land has been given to the states. In some cases, Federal land has been secured. Increasingly, however, states are finding it necessary to buy their land.

Some state park systems have found an answer to the problem by charging fees to help meet expenses and finance improvements. Some authorities feel that, although fees should be kept at a minimum, at least 50 per cent of the cost should be borne by the park users. The sources of funds commonly employed are gate fees, charges for automobile stickers that admit visitors to all parks in a given state, parking fees, admission charges for the use of special facilities such as swimming pools, and returns from concession operations.

State Forests

State forests were originally reserved principally for the production of timber, although watershed protection was also important. In many cases cutover lands and abandoned farms that no one else wanted were acquired. The reforestation of these lands through artificial or natural means not only increased timber resources but also protected watersheds and prevented further land deterioration.

Just as state parks preceded national parks, state forests preceded national forests. As early as 1867, when Wyoming appointed a forest inquiry commission, states showed interest in the preservation of trees. In 1885, six years before the national forest system began, New York created, in the Adirondacks, the first state forest preserve. California, Colorado, and Ohio established forestry departments that same year. During the next fifteen years, several other states followed suit.

State forests and related lands totaled 19.3 million acres in 1956, not including the forests in state park lands. Most of this acreage was commercial timber-producing land. Five of the states held three fourths of all state forestry acreage. They were Minnesota, Michigan, New York, Pennsylvania, and Washington.

Though less developed, state forests are much more extensive in area than state parks. State forests have always received a certain amount of recreational use and today most of the forest areas are open for recreation. A brief description of some of the recreational uses of state forests follows.

Hunting and Fishing. Unlike state parks, state forests are usually open to hunting, at least in certain areas. Fishing is likewise usually permitted, and provisions often are made for boat rental and private-boat launching.

Camping and Picnicking. Day-use areas for picnickers and casual visitors are increasing in numbers. Camping areas for families and, in some cases, leases for resident youth camps, are available. Much of the growth of family camping in recent years has taken place on state forest lands.

Summer Homes. Sites are leased for summer homes in some state forests.

Other Activities. Hiking, sightseeing, horseback riding, sailing, swimming, canoeing, boating, and skiing are accommodated in state forests. . . .

State Fish and Game Agencies

The management of wildlife resources, the protection of fish and game, and, in some cases, the provision of public hunting and fishing grounds are major recreation responsibilities. For the most part, these are responsibilities of the states. Unlike other resources, wildlife does not belong to the private landholders but, rather, to the state. Wildlife that crosses state and international boundaries is the concern of the Federal Government, and, therefore, migratory birds are under the joint control of the state and the nation.

All states have some state machinery to handle the problems of wildlife. California and New Hampshire were the first to establish fish and game commissions (1878); . . . other states soon followed. In some states, the responsibility is divided among two or more agencies, although more commonly a department of fish and game is the single authority.

All states are faced with difficult problems connected with the protection and management of wildlife habitats. Many of these problems arise out of the popularity of hunting and fishing. The numbers of hunters and fishermen are growing rapidly at the same time that industry, highways, homes, and agriculture are pre-empting the natural habitats of fish and game. The problem of retaining sufficient land and water areas and managing them in the interests of sportsmen has become difficult. Some states have embarked on programs of expanding public fishing and hunting areas. Sometimes these are state forest lands, but more frequently they are lands administered by state fish and game agencies. Occasionally, private land is under public lease to provide areas. Through stocking and planting of fish and game and through the management of the lands and waters to provide food and cover, the state endeavors to improve hunting and fishing in places open to the general public.

The Federal Government cooperates in improving habitat through the provisions of several acts of Congress, notably the Pittman-Robertson Act of 1937 and the Dingell-Johnson Act of 1950. The former provides for a tax on firearms and ammunition, the proceeds of which are distributed to the states on the basis of the numbers of hunting licenses issued. The money is used for the improvement of habitats and the development of special wildlife areas. Some funds go to private landholders for the improvement of wildlife population by plantings in special, protected areas. The Dingell-Johnson Act provides for a tax on fishing tackle, and the funds made available therefrom are granted to the states for the improvement of fishing.

One of the most difficult problems related to wildlife is that private lands have been increasingly closed to sportsmen, largely as a result of a few sportsmen's lack of consideration. Private land is, however, a major wildlife habitat in most parts of the country. Numerous steps have been taken by state fish and game authorities to open private lands to the public and to make them more productive of wildlife.

Commercial fishing and trapping are regulated in all states. The growing competition between commercial interests and the sportsmen often results in conflicts difficult to resolve. The state must give consideration to the man who makes a living from these activities, while at the same time satisfying the demands of sportsmen.

Most states maintain fish hatcheries and game farms. They provide seed stock when certain species have become depleted and in some cases plant fish in areas in which there is extremely heavy fishing. Financial support for these programs comes largely from hunting and fishing license fees. . . .

Protection and improvement of wildlife depend upon research. Research programs are usually carried on by state fish and game agencies in cooperation with educational institutions.

It is only through the most strenuous efforts of propagation, habitat improvement, legal control, and public education that wildlife can be assured for future generations. In the future, more emphasis must be placed upon the enjoyment of wildlife without destroying it. It is possible that hunting can be provided in years to come for only a small percentage of people and that hunting with field glasses and cameras will for most people replace hunting with guns.

THE FCC AND TELEVISION [8]

This is my third annual talk with you as FCC [Federal Communications Commission] chairman. Let us review together some of the more important developments of the past several years.

First, in 1961, it was predicted that international television "will be with us soon." Soon came much sooner than expected, on July 10, 1962. . . . An active communications satellite was launched through the joint efforts of government and private initiative, with a license from the FCC.

Already we have seen, live, the Ecumenical Conference, the midnight sun in Sweden, fishermen in Sicily, night life in Paris. Europeans have glimpsed the Statue of Liberty, the United Nations, the Rio Grande, and a big league baseball game. The day was brought closer when billions of people on this planet will be linked through instantaneous sight and sound. . . .

Second, educational television. You were promised that "if there is not a nationwide educational television system in this country, it will not be the fault of the FCC." A strong national educational television system is steadily developing because ETV now is receiving more of the necessary support from leaders in education, in government, in business, and in the general community and I'm proud to say from many of you.

Since January 1961, we have reserved fifty-six additional channels for educational use, and laid the basis for a number of statewide systems. Twenty-three more ETV stations are on the

[8] From " 'Mind-Forged Manacles,' " address by Newton N. Minow, former chairman, Federal Communications Commission, to the National Association of Broadcasters on April 2, 1963. Published in *Equal Time*, by Newton N. Minow. p 246-61. Copyright © 1964 by Newton N. Minow. Reprinted by permission of Atheneum Publishers. New York.

air now than two years ago, bringing the total of today's stations on the air to seventy-seven. This is only the beginning. . . .

Third, as you were promised, renewals of broadcast licenses have not been automatic. In the last two years, fourteen licenses were revoked or denied a renewal. Fifteen more are now in the hearing process on the question of revocation or renewal. Twenty-six licenses were granted on a short-term basis. Notices of Apparent Liability for fines have been issued in twenty-one cases. In fourteen hearings involving license renewal or revocation, the hearing was ordered held in the station's own community.

Some hearings have also been held in the field to give the public a chance to express views on local service. These hearings have been conducted without regard to renewals of licenses. The public, your real ownership, has had an opportunity to give its views—some good, some bad—and to participate to a fuller extent in your decisions on broadcast service. I believe that with broadcasting stations, as with income-tax returns, the practice of making an occasional audit in depth is an effective though sometimes painful way of finding out whether the public interest is being served. I cannot understand how local expression about broadcasting service can be interpreted as governmental interference with freedom. The public's right to insist on having a voice in your decisions will be honored and maintained.

Some people in this industry have been finding out that when they promise public service to obtain a valuable license, they will be held to their promise. And the large majority of you . . . silently—I repeat, silently—endorse our efforts.

Fourth, we have encouraged you to take positions on issues, to be unafraid of controversy, to editorialize, to help mold and lead public opinion. More and more of you are beginning to use your voices and to take a stand on such adult themes as foreign aid, Cuba, civil rights, narcotics addiction, and the tax program.

Where there have been complaints, the commission has backed you up, provided that you afforded a reasonable opportunity for the presentation of opposing views. We have repeatedly protected you against those who would water down your convictions through pressure-group intimidation or suppress your freedom through commercial reprisals. And I might add that when the going gets rough on true issues of freedom of expression, many of you otherwise staunch defenders of free speech are conspicuously silent and absent from the fray.

Fifth, you were promised that we would press the FCC Network Study to a conclusion with useful results. This study . . . [begun in 1955] has now been completed. Our staff has made a report on network policies and practices, which the Congress is printing and distributing. We now have a clearer picture of the function, the power and the problems of television network operations.

The basic issue before us can be stated quickly. The networks are an indispensable part of television. Our three networks have furnished to the people of this nation informational and entertainment programing which could not otherwise have been achieved. Strong networks—and I hope one day there will be more than only three—are essential to successful television broadcasting. But when does strength become all-embracing dominance? Not long ago, an executive of one of the country's largest television advertisers, David J. Mahoney of Colgate-Palmolive, said:

> While the number of men who comprise the television industry may be relatively small, there is nothing small nor unimportant about the power this body wields. The networks today not only determine what gets on the air, but they own practically all of the shows. I believe there are about a dozen exceptions, but even in some of these, the networks have partial or controlling interests.

Power inevitably carries with it grave responsibility. We presently look to the stations, not the networks, while we know that it is generally the networks and not the stations which make the crucial decisions about what the public sees and hears. The responsibility for what goes out *over* the air cannot be left up *in* the air. And those who are making a buck from television must stop passing the buck.

Our problem is to maintain a free market for ideas in television, while preserving and encouraging essential services which only the networks currently provide. The ultimate solutions may rest with the Congress. . . .

I would like today to make several suggestions for all of us concerned with television. We can all agree that one of TV's basic problems is the insatiable appetite of the medium for programing material. Given the best talent, the best intent and the best financing, it is difficult for TV to create quality programing at the fantastic rate programs are consumed. One of the tragedies of television today is that most of our great programs, just like our not-so-great, disappear after one fleeting hour or half hour, never to be seen again. . . . A great deal of superlative TV fare . . . can certainly be repeated on the new UHF [Ultra-High-Frequency] channels for the public. With some imagination and enterprise, UHF in the future can, among its other useful potentials, provide the ideal second and third opportunities for the great hours and half hours of TV. . . . The heavy cost of producing much of our top TV demands residual uses to amortize production expenses, uses over and above the sometime syndication or sale of foreign rights. The present system often produces a colossal waste—of money, of talent, and of dedicated work. It results in a shameful deprivation, a needless withholding of information and entertainment from what is probably the majority audience who missed the first showing.

What can UHF do to help? Quite a bit. UHF could make it possible for the networks to have two affiliates in some communities, a first-run and a second-run affiliate. The second affiliate would be a UHF station which would have access to the network's programs on a delay or repeat basis. The public would then have a second chance to see the best the networks have to offer within a week or so for timeless drama, music, and entertainment programs, and perhaps a shorter time in the case of news or informational programs.

Consider the benefits. New, less affluent advertisers could enter television; program costs could be better amortized; participants could receive some additional income. Even as I point out these pleasant economic consequences, I am aware that there are a lot of cloudy problems. You will wonder about competing with yourselves. What about sponsors? What about ratings? About unions? As cloudy as the problems are, equally clear is one overriding consideration: your responsibility to the public.

That responsibility . . . can be met by shaking those mind-forged manacles and by breaking through the crusty rigidity and stubborn complacency of the status quo. Perhaps you have some better ideas on how to accomplish the same purposes. How about some experiments? UHF in the future offers a rare second chance, an end to the scarcity of air time that has plagued television in the past. Let us use this exceptional opportunity to try out some new ideas. . . . The new channels also provide fresh opportunities to see programs from other lands. Fine television fare is being produced all over the world, and their producers are eager to make these programs available to the American audience. . . .

Another subject we should discuss is commercials, a matter of debate in broadcasting since 1922. It was in 1922 that Herbert Hoover, then responsible, as Secretary of Commerce, for the regulation of broadcasting, said, "It is inconceivable that we should allow so great a possibility for service, for news, for entertainment, for education, and for vital commercial purposes to be drowned in advertising chatter." Forty-one years later, the American public is drowning, and calling for help. A television commercial is broadcast somewhere in the United States every 1.7 seconds. . . .

At the FCC, we have a policy against "overcommercialization." If you ask us what that means, we would have to confess that in all its years, the FCC has never established ground rules defining it.

However, at the NAB [National Association of Broadcasters] you have a Code of Broadcasting Practices. In the code is a specific and detailed provision for time to be devoted to commercials. The code was written by this industry and represents the thinking of responsible broadcasters about advertising practices. In your view, it establishes a fair standard under which "revenues from advertising" can support "the free, competitive American system of broadcasting" and at the same time "make available to the eyes and ears of the American people the finest programs of information, education, culture, and entertainment." Those quotations are from the preamble to the code itself.

The trouble with that code provision is that it is not complied with and is not adequately enforced. According to your own Robert Swezey, the head of your Code Authority, "It is virtually impossible for us to maintain industry standards in any practical sense. The public is still being victimized by the poor programing and shoddy practices of a large element of the industry which has no interest in standards and no compulsion to observe them."

The NAB itself says that only 1750 radio stations subscribe to the code, approximately 38 per cent of the radio stations on the air. In television, the figures are 405 subscribers, approximately 70 per cent of the television stations. And even those who subscribe to the codes do not always adhere to its provisions. . . .

Last year, I quoted . . . Mr. Swezey, who said to you that the time had come "to put up or shut up about self-regulation." I submit you have succeeded in doing neither. . . .

I would urge that the law require that every broadcaster belong to the NAB, just as most brokers belong to the National Association of Securities Dealers. You should be professionals, a status which many in your ranks already deserve. But this demands that you maintain high standards and that you discipline those among you who repeatedly cut corners. . . .

I urge that you have the lawful authority to enforce your own commercial standards, with an appeal to the FCC, just as is done in the securities field with the SEC [Securities and Exchange Commission]. I cannot understand why you do not see the wisdom of taking such a course instead of requiring further action from the Government. . . .

There have been improvements in broadcasting. Many of you are doing a better job of serving the public than was the case several years ago. . . . In the area of information programing, there are many reasons to be proud. A comparison of today's television schedules with those of three years ago will indicate there is now slightly more than three times as much informational programing in evening hours. . . .

I have been urging you to see if there was not more room on television "to teach, to inform, to stretch, to enlarge the capacities of our children." You have found a bit more room for some exceptional programs. Some of you may ask now in the words of the familiar political slogan, "Had enough?" The Answer is "Positively No!" Nothing is enough, nothing is too good for the children who spend seventy million hours a day with you. You're beginning to demonstrate what television can do. . . . As you meet your responsibility, you will remember to provide more news and public affairs programs where ideas are rubbed against other ideas into the friction of controversy. On such informational programs may rest the strengthening of an enlightened electorate, critical to the survival of freedom. But you will also remember that you need to do more than feed our minds. Broadcasting must also nourish our spirit. We need entertainment which helps us to grow in compassion and understanding.

III. THE USES OF LEISURE

EDITOR'S INTRODUCTION

One of the criteria by which a society may be judged is its forms of recreation. The values it cherishes, the traditions it continues, the responsibilities it accepts, the satisfactions it derives—all of these find expression in its recreational behavior.

At the present time Americans at leisure conform to work habits. Their pastimes usually involve action, motion, competition, and achievement. Free time is often devoted to taking a course or gaining proficiency in a sport. Like work, recreation is largely organized or controlled—by a commercial enterprise, a government unit, or a private organization. A camping trip often involves arranging months in advance for reservations and staying at a site maintained by a government agency that also enforces rules and regulations. Americans in large numbers register for a bus or bus-plane tour, and a business enterprise plans all restaurant, hotel, and sightseeing stops.

Within this institutionalized framework Americans have the widest and fullest and most varied opportunities to fill their leisure hours. Mass media, books, spectator sports, participant sports, social service, civic service, political activity, adult education, motor trips, the fine arts, loafing, and conversation are among the general categories from which Americans can pick and choose.

This section is a review of some forms of recreation in present-day American life. Certain sporting activities are considered by Arnold Hano, Leonard Koppett, Reuel Denney, and W. Clifford Harvey, and various forms of camping are surveyed by H. Dan Corbin, Dorothea Graham, and a group of campers themselves. America's most popular pastime is pleasure driving; Eunice T. Juckett reports on her transcontinental motor vacation in the summer of 1964. The use of leisure time for community service is illustrated by James Nathan Miller's article.

One of the results of increased leisure has been an increase in reading. The multiplication of libraries, the growth of book clubs, and the publication of paperbacks have also contributed considerably to the boom in reading, which is surveyed by Helen B. Shaffer. The concluding article is a poet's lamentation on the effects of the mass media on the arts. Other social observers, for example Bruce Bliven in the first article in this book, presents a somewhat brighter view of the state of culture in contemporary America. (This subject is dealt with at greater length in *Culture in America*, edited by Vineta Colby—The Reference Shelf, Vol. 36, No. 1.)

JE-NE-SAIS-QUOITS OR HORSESHOES? [1]

The style-consciousness that pervades life in America today does not exclude the world of sport. We have chic sports, and not so chic sports; sports that have élan—in a word, that are "in" —and sports that are oafish, games for clods. On one hand, it might be said, there is *je-ne-sais-quoits;* on the other hand, horseshoes.

The prime requisite of an "in" sport is snob appeal. It is a game the smart set plays. Everyone has his own idea of who—or what—the smart set is and one man's opinion, in this context, is as good as another's. What follows, then, is The Complete Guide to Chic Sports. It is unofficial, yes, but very correct. Those who demur at the findings can go fly a kite. (Kite-flying is "out.")

The chic seven, among participant sports, are boating, surfing, skiing, flying, sky diving, pocket billiards and squash. (Strangely enough, there are virtually no spectator sports today that are "in." The only one that comes readily to mind is watching the New York Giants football team on a motel television set seventy-five miles from New York.)

Boating has been "in" ever since American sea dogs licked the British in the American Revolution and the War of 1812. We are still stirred by the cool smugness of "We have met the enemy

[1] From article by Arnold Hano, sportswriter. New York *Times Magazine.* p 96+. S. 13, '64. © 1964 by The New York Times Company. Reprinted by permission.

and they are ours" and "I have not yet begun to fight." It is important to note, however, that the boats upon which these heroes stood when they made these statements were sailboats. Motorboats—or "stinkpots," as they are affectionately described by the cognoscenti of sail—are "out." The sailing craft, whether dinghy or racing yacht, is a true snob symbol. Spinnaker . . . topgallant . . . Sir Thomas Lipton . . . catamaran. The mind reels.

(John F. Kennedy, of course, added great luster to sailing, just as Teddy Roosevelt elevated wrestling and hunting, and William Howard Taft helped make golf "in" before Eisenhower and his business cronies made it "out.")

Surfing, with its connotations of having been the sport of ancient Hawaiian kings, is rapidly becoming very "in." The fact that it is more or less limited to the coasts of Peru, Brazil, Hawaii, Mexico, Australia and California (although Asbury Park—in New Jersey, of all places—and Long Island's Gilgo Beach are horning in on the sport) adds to the image. Surfing is an "in" sport that is a cult. The language of the fans contains words like *rocker, skags, green water, soup, mushing-out* and *hang ten* (meaning that one stands up front, with all one's toes curled over the nose of the board). It is also a sport that attracts a great deal of special wardrobe, and a dance has been named in its honor.

Skiing, although its roots are much more prosaic than surfing (one has images of Lapps flapping around on barrel staves), has been, and still is, "in." Sixty years ago . . . the sport's devotees were limited to a few Scandinavian colonies in the Midwest. Since then it has spread a good distance east and west. Skiing is not only a cult; it is a Way of Life. The editors of *Ski Life,* a magazine, have referred to it as the "constant pursuit of an ideal," as an "atavistic desire to fling one's self against nature," and as "a blinding flash of accomplishment, which comes on a crystal-like day. . . ."

Like surfing, skiing is fraught with fashions and special equipment, and non-skiers are happy to stay at least one pole's length away.

There are two new participant sports that have all the earmarks of becoming truly "in." One is flying one's own airplane —not to business engagements, but to a distant fishing hole or a choice beach. Or just for fun. (There are 8,000 airfields available to these gentlemen fliers, who may pilot Piper Cubs, priced at about $2,000 or twin-engined Aero Grand Commanders, about $146,000. The size of the plane makes no difference to the air-minded anyway. Fliers have the same democratic instincts as Virginia fox-hunters—which is to say they treat each other as equals, and no one else.)

Even newer is sky diving, the delicate art of flinging oneself from an airplane and indulging in free fall (which is just what it sounds like) until such time as the faller decides it's time to pull his ripcord. At first, sky divers seemed a rough bunch with suicidal tendencies that would have awed Freud. Today, the sport is smoothing out. Parachute centers are thriving and when the clientele rids itself of some of the less chic impedimenta (jukeboxes and drinks named Leaping Lena) the sport should become something to be reckoned with.

Indoors, it's pocket billiards, formerly "pool." They knew what they were doing when they changed the name. You shot "pool" in an undershirt; you play "pocket billiards" in soup-and-fish. And today's tables are outfitted in handsome pastels—tangerine, beige, chartreuse.

Finally, there is squash, the most "in" of all participant sports, a game so secretive only its few university-club buffs have ever seen it. This is true "in-ness." It is a sport that has practically no literature; it needs to blow no horn. It is elusive, glamorous, solitary. For all anybody knows, it may no longer be played.

What sports are "out"? Where *won't* you find the smart set these days? Well, you won't find them fishing for trout (although they might be having a crack at black bass). Or hunting. Even fox-hunting has had it. P. G. Wodehouse pointed out recently that there hasn't been a fox-hunting joke in Punch in five years. "More and more people," he wrote, "are beginning to realize that fox-hunting is a foolish pastime and that just the same   thrills can be had from swatting flies." Fly-swatting, Wodehouse suggests, may be our next "in" sport.

Bowling has become a financial success and so cannot be "in." The fifty-mile walk enjoyed a vogue mercifully even briefer than miniature golf. Golf's pretentiousness overcomes the fringe benefits of conviviality at the nineteenth hole. Tennis, once very U, lost caste when bulldozers ripped up those lovely lawn courts; you can't look very smart on asphalt. Besides, after a tennis match you drink iced tea. Instant. Volleyball is "in" on Fire Island, but absolutely nowhere else.

What's ahead? Tomorrow's chic sport may be one of those parochial pastimes to which a few remain stubbornly devoted while all about go ape for hockey. Perhaps status will befall the man who enters an ostrich in the annual ostrich and camel races at Indio, California; or he who joins the pack-burro derby in Colorado (you don't ride the beast; you pull or push him twenty-three miles through the Rockies).

There are whale-blubber-eating contests in Alaska; chariot races in Cascade, Idaho; crossbow tourneys in Huntsville, Arkansas. And Californians go down to the beaches on moonlight nights to hunt the elusive grunion—a skinny, silvery, smeltlike fish who comes in on one wave, lays her eggs on the sand, and escapes with the next wave. You catch grunion by hand, if you ever see one. There are people who insist that grunion do not exist. Perhaps this is already the truest of "in" sports. You have nothing to show for it. (Trophies are out.)

THE EX-NATIONAL SPORT [2]

Major league baseball, a mass spectator sport still steeped in its nineteenth century origins, is suffering today from that most modern of twentieth century maladies: "bad image." The illness has occurred relatively recently. Until a decade ago few people bothered to challenge baseball's right to a place alongside Mom,

[2] From "The Ex-National Sport Looks to Its Image," by Leonard Koppett, New York Times sports reporter. New York Times Magazine. p 18-19+. D. 20, '64. © 1964 by The New York Times Company. Reprinted by permission.

apple pie and freedom of assembly. There were those who didn't care, but not many who did failed to accept baseball as a peculiar, indigenous and vaguely defined "special" element in the fabric of American culture.

Today this favored position is not merely challenged—it has disappeared. While millions of people still feel a passionate interest in every sort of baseball news, fewer and fewer regard it as essentially different from other forms of entertainment. Even baseball's own hierarchy admits that the aura has gone, or is going. Commissioner Ford C. Frick, in a top-secret report to the twenty major-league club owners last month [November 1964] in Phoenix, spelled out the "bad image" problem and blamed the owners for it. . . .

Baseball Yesterday

What was the baseball of the "old days" like, before the "image" got tarnished? Well, a generation ago it would have sounded sacrilegious to identify the sport as "part of the *entertainment* industry." (Today, of course, that very phrase is used to justify the purchase of the New York Yankees by the Columbia Broadcasting System.) A fan attended an event, not a performance. He had as little interest in—and awareness of—the commercial background of the goings-on on the field as the audience at a concert or opera has of the financial problems involved in a musical evening.

The supply of heroes seemed endless: Mathewson, Johnson, Cobb, Ruth. These, and a hundred others slightly less famous, were not merely great ball players; each had a distinct character in the eye of the fan. This character did not always coincide with the man in real life, but it was clear-cut, consistent, identifiable and human.

The fan, a generation ago, believed that victory on the field was the most important thing in the world to all those concerned with baseball. And he was deeply loyal to locale. He knew that the players who wore, let's say, a Brooklyn uniform were recruited from all over the country, but as long as they wore it, they were part of Brooklyn. To a great extent the prominent players did become a part of the community they played in. They settled in the residential neighborhoods that surrounded the ball parks built in the early years of the century; they frequented local restaurants, shops (yes, bars, too); they mingled with the fans entering and leaving the park.

Consider, for example, Ebbets Field. The structure was small, the stands close to the foul lines and the sense of intimacy very great. A fan yelling "Throw him a fish!" when Lonnie Frey booted a ball at shortstop could be heard clearly throughout the park. Players' shouts at one another could be heard, too.

When a man came to a game—a *day* game—he brought his children, who became converts. Older children could come by themselves—after school in spring and fall, to double-headers in summer. Relatively few seats were boxes and almost any location in the park was available the day of a game. In such surroundings, the Dodgers could, and did, become national as well as civic celebrities. Their "daffiness," their overpopulation of third base, their brushes with death from fly balls to the head were known to baseball fans everywhere. When they got into a fight (which Red Barber, their radio announcer, established once and for all as a "rhubarb"), no one could help taking sides. . . .

Later, when the Dodgers had earned the affectionate title of "Bums," they started to win pennants. They became the epitome of the successful underdog. The love lavished on Pee Wee Reese, Jackie Robinson, Gil Hodges, Roy Campanella and the others of the postwar era was a beautiful thing.

In 1948, when Leo Durocher switched from managing the Dodgers to managing the Giants, the sense of shock was as real as if an Englishman had been suddenly elected premier of France. When the lights were turned out at Ebbets Field and 30,000 fans lit matches to simulate a birthday cake for Pee Wee Reese, it was a press-agent-instigated idea, yes, but instigated by a press agent in tune with the populace.

When the Dodgers won the 1941 pennant, their first in twenty-one years, fans marched across Brooklyn Bridge and stood for hours on West Forty-second Street, booing the darkened offices of the Yankees, whom they would play in the World Series.

Baseball Today

And what is it like today? The Dodgers have ceased to exist, although there is a team by that name playing in a place called Los Angeles. At the new Dodger Stadium, almost half the seats are boxes. A man is more likely to bring a client than a son. (This is even more true at Yankee Stadium today.) The players, having become members of the upper middle class, live in suburban communities twenty and thirty miles away; they are scattered and the community life in which they take part is suburban, not *local* in the fans' sense of the term.

Inside the Los Angeles park, the customer can get dinner, plenty of liquor, souvenirs by the dozen, a host of special services—all far removed from the hot dogs and peanuts that used to represent the limit of ball park fare. This makes him more comfortable, and probably overweight, and it also drives home the point that his money is being sought at every turn.

Where have the fans' illusions that baseball was "something special" gone? How could they be maintained for half a century, then eroded in the last five years? The steps are easy to identify. First, by yielding to the pressure (perhaps unavoidable) for unlimited night games, the majors gave up one of their distinctive characteristics. The difference between a night game and a day game may be hard to define, but it's easy to feel: the one connotes sport, the other performance; one belongs to the young of all ages, the other to seekers of entertainment. A few night games were attractive galas, like extra Sundays or holidays; a steady diet undermined one psychological prop of the "something special" illusion. Then, by jumping franchises in all directions for the avowed purpose of making more money, baseball destroyed the very stability, statistical validity and competitive integrity that made the game so attractive.

Between 1903, when the American League solidified and won major status, and 1953, when the Braves moved from Boston to Milwaukee, the major league structure stood as a monument to security in a frightening, changing world. The same sixteen teams, located in only eleven cities with fairly compact travel connections, played a similar schedule pattern year after year, creating records that could be compared and discussed. What changes occurred were few, minor and easily understood.

The first few franchise shifts did not have an immediately disastrous effect. But then, in 1957, the point of no return was reached when, after months of rumors and denials, the Dodgers and Giants were moved to Los Angeles and San Francisco. The moving of these teams to new towns tore the fabric of stability beyond repair. If Brooklyn could be deprived of its Dodgers, if the Giants of McGraw could leave Broadway, if all the accumulated tradition could be brushed aside, the fan could feel no more sure of his baseball than of anything else in a bewildering universe.

And again, details were disturbing. All sorts of regulations had to be rewritten to make the shifts legal, even in baseball terms. The Dodgers had to play (for four years, it turned out) in a football stadium with 90,000 seats but no suitable playing field. The Pacific Coast League, highest of the minor leagues, had its status summarily destroyed. Coast-to-coast travel was required of players with no essential change in schedule patterns. In other words, honorable business dealings and decent conditions for playing the games had to be sacrificed for potential profit.

The next step was expansion. In the fall of 1960, the American League decided to go to ten teams immediately; the National League would do so in 1962. This was organized baseball's answer to a proposed third major league, to be called the Continental. After tossing up roadblocks of one sort and another, the majors finally decided to take in what appeared to be the strongest members of the developing league. This killed third-league talk. Only one of the Continental groups—the New York Mets—actually wound up with a franchise.

To stock the four new clubs, the existing teams supplied one hundred of the least desirable players on their rosters for a total of about $8 million. In other words, the initiation fee for each newcomer was something over $2 million; the profit for each existing club was about $600,000. And, competitively speaking, the talent supplied, with few exceptions, was practically worthless. All this, of course, received extensive press coverage, and its effect on baseball's image as a sport need not be belabored.

Expansion also meant ten-team leagues, playing 162-game schedules, with back-breaking travel. There were two serious drawbacks to this scheme. One is that a ten-team league is bottom-heavy with also-rans; a contending team can play only two ninths of its games with other contenders (that is, the top three teams in the standings at any given time).

The other is that all the records and statistics, so precious a part of baseball lore, were compromised, and events conspired to underline this point immediately. In 1961, Roger Maris of the Yankees hit sixty-one home runs, breaking Babe Ruth's record; but instead of being hailed as the most glamorous of all baseball feats, this only generated arguments about the validity of records made in 162-game schedules vs. 154-game schedules.

Meanwhile, the players themselves were doing their share to disillusion the fan. When they achieved a fabulous pension plan, financed by World Series television income, most fans identified with them and cheered; when they foisted a second all-star game on the public to increase pension funds, they revealed themselves in a mercenary light. . . .

Baseball's increasing dependence on radio and television income has also helped prevent the creation of illusion, especially in children. Messages selling beer and cigarettes, delivered twenty times per game, day after day, may or may not be desirable from any of a dozen points of view; they definitely do not, however, instill an image of pure sport. Radio had been a help to baseball, whetting the appetite of the true fan, keeping him informed and making new addicts. Television, however, was a short-term bonanza leading to long-term disaster which is only now beginning to be recognized.

The trouble with television is that it exists. It creates a demand for the one big thing, seen now, by everybody, everywhere, and makes any sort of minor-league operation difficult. The major leagues, however, were not content to let attrition take its course, let alone develop a plan for combating it: they piped major league games into minor league territories and promptly killed off the minors then and there. The main thing is that a baseball game on television remains a television show: it may make some baseball addicts, but it certainly makes more television addicts. Thus, one more distinguishing feature of baseball is removed and it becomes "just another entertainment."

Other problems, which the fan did not seek out, were thrown into his illusion-making machinery. The congressional hearings about whether or not baseball (and other sports) should be granted specific antitrust exemptions contributed a great deal of illusion-wrecking information and speculation. Congress still hasn't taken any action, but exactly how much business and how little sport there is in today's corporate-structure, tax-conscious, peripheral-income-oriented baseball "clubs" has been spelled out too often to be ignored. And the unprecedented increase in shifting of players, stimulated by expansion corroded much fan identification. By June 1962, the turnover of personnel on all major league rosters in the preceding twelve months exceeded 50 per cent.

All these factors, then, bruised baseball's image and robbed it of its special status. The events of 1964 knocked the image flat on its back. Chief among them was the purchase of the Yankees in August by CBS for $14.2 million. There was talk of conflict of interest; antitrust action seemed possible; for weeks the papers were full of stories about why the deal might be a bad thing. Aside from anything else, it certainly tied baseball closer to the "entertainment industry"; in fact, both the Yankees and CBS boasted of this.

In October, the Braves decided to move to Atlanta, having milked Milwaukee dry. (Attendance, after an average of 2 million a year for seven years, had dropped to under 1 million in the last three.) The avowed reason: Atlanta had a better TV-market-area potential! Milwaukee authorities went to court to make the Braves stay. The National League ordered them to stay, then approved the move for 1966, and a lease with Atlanta's new stadium was signed. Milwaukee citizens insist they'll find another big league team to come to Milwaukee by then. (It might be Cleveland, which after much consideration of Seattle, Oakland and Dallas, decided to stay in Cleveland "for one more year," and perhaps longer, if the citizens bestir themselves to buy enough tickets.)

It is no wonder, then, that in November even Frick, who had never before shown the slightest inclination to rock a boat, told the owners off, stating that "baseball people are unwilling to abide by the rules which they themselves make" and that "expediency is permitted to replace sound judgment." It was, in a sense, a farewell gesture. He will retire from his $65,000-a-year job next October [1965] after fourteen years.

Can anything be done? Not really. Public relations consultants may be called in (they have been called in before, without effect), and Frick's suggestion that the commissioner be given greater powers—like those possessed by the late Judge Kenesaw Mountain Landis, who ruled baseball with an iron hand until 1945—was adopted at the winter meetings. However, the effectiveness of any such change in powers will be wholly dependent on how strong a man the owners choose—in other words, want— as their next commissioner.

The only real change on the horizon is further expansion. Within a few years, the leagues will probably expand to twelve teams, playing in six-team subdivisions. Thus, six teams in the western half of the National League may play one another twenty times each, and the six in the eastern half nine times a year, with all games counting in the standings, but with two separate standings. This would mean a 154-game schedule, with two divisional pennant races and no team ever lower than sixth. The divisional winners would play off for the right to go into the World Series against the American League winner, determined the same way.

This particular case of expansion will help. It will cut travel, heighten fan interest in pennant races, remove the bottom layer of dead weight and improve statistics. But it will not restore baseball to the unique position it once held. Nothing will. Times, as even the owners and Frick have finally admitted, change.

Baseball seems destined to remain a profitable, respected, important segment of the mass entertainment industry, a growing field. It will still command a certain number of fanatics. But it must share billing with pro football, and with television it simply cannot compete.

For the average fan, something has gone out of the game; or rather, come into it: a wariness that makes total emotional commitment difficult. Years ago, a columnist commented on the coldly efficient, perpetually victorious Yankees: "Rooting for the Yankees is like rooting for U.S. Steel." Now the joke has become a reality, and it's pretty hard to root for a business—especially a business that may move away when a better offer comes along.

The old fan's motto might have been: "My ball club, right or wrong, but right or wrong, my ball club still." Today's fan had better feel: "Eat, drink (beer), smoke (the right brand) and make merry—for tomorrow they may move the franchise." And if that be bad image, perhaps baseball had better make the most of it.

IN PRAISE OF HOT-RODDING [3]

What do people do when they are not satisfied with the movies and TV and when they react against merely spectatorial relationships to the world of sport? They make things, or they participate in some sort of performance or contest themselves. This might be the place, therefore, to reconsider such things as the little-theater movement in the United States or the rise of the amateur musical performing groups to numbers unheard of a generation ago. However, these developments have been studied before; they are not essentially new; and they are not fully popular. To speak in terms of the mass culture and its audience competency, it would be more germane to find, if we could, an activity which involves a wide range of economic groups, which

[3] Reprinted from *The Astonished Muse* by Reuel Denney by permission of The University of Chicago Press. © 1957 by The University of Chicago. p 32-3, 138-56. Reuel Denney is professor of social sciences, University of Chicago.

hooks into the major daily consumption patterns of the nation, and which has had a powerful amateur influence on the professionals in its own field. In the past twenty years, hardly any activity of this sort is so worthy of notice as hot-rodding, with its manifold implications for the place of the auto and automotive craftsmanship in American life. Here, then, is a case study of a group of Participative Purists.

Images of Competence

A general early public image of the hot-rodder is crystallized in a statement made in 1950 by Thomas W. Ryan, director of the New York Division of Safety:

Possession of the "hot rod" car is presumptive evidence of an intent to speed. . . . Speed is Public Enemy No. 1 of the highways. It is obvious that a driver of a "hot rod" car has an irresistible temptation to "step on it" and accordingly operate the vehicle in a reckless manner endangering human life. It also shows a deliberate and premeditated idea to violate the law. These vehicles are largely improvised by home mechanics and are capable of high speed and dangerous maneuverability. They have therefore become a serious menace to the safe movement of traffic. The operators of these cars are confused into believing that driving is a competitive sport. They have a feeling of superiority in recklessly darting in and out of traffic in their attempt to outspeed other cars, on the road. . . .

In an article for the *American Quarterly* Eugene Balsley, a former hot-rodder turned reporter on the fad, showed that the hot-rodder's picture of himself was quite different. He reported:

. . . A hot rod accident or incident is newsworthy, while an accident involving ordinary cars is so common that it is usually not newspaperworthy. We wonder whether you appreciate the real contribution that the hot rod industry, for it is an industry, has made to automotive transportation. The automotive industry has the equivalent of a milliondollar experimental laboratory in the hot rod industry from which they can get valuable technical information free of any expense or risk of reputation. . . .

Balsley documented the degree to which the hot-rodder and his friends were highly articulate in their criticism of the Detroit automobile, with scorn for "the Deroit solution of a problem in transportation, engineering, aesthetics." Hot-rodders asserted that Detroit's mass-production car was uneconomical, unsafe at modern road speeds, and uglier than it had any right to be; they added that it was too costly, too heavy, and too complicated by class and status symbolism to be a good car. The hot-rodder's credo, that driving should not be so effortless that one forgets one is driving until after the crash, was another ground for rejecting the Detroit car.

When the hot rodder rebuilds a Detroit car to his own design [wrote Balsley] he is aiming to create a car which is a magical and vibrant thing. Yet, back of his dream design we can see the workings of the practical engineering standards that dominate the hot-rod culture. There are sound reasons for the hot-rod builder's selection and rejection of various components of the Detroit car. Any given car, when rebuilt by a hot rodder, can be loosely assigned to one of four classes of design. . . .

Cars rebuilt by means of the simplest changes can be classed in the fourth rank. The owner in this category changes only the exterior of the body. He is, unfortunately, aided by the countless manufacturers of doll-up accessories. . . .

Transformation in cars of the next higher rank, the third, are dictated by consideration of function, although ornamentation may still be used. While in cars of the lowest category the engine remains substantially unaltered, the engines of next-higher-rank cars are changed in order to increase horsepower and acceleration. . . .

When we move up to the second highest rank, we cross the line into the true mysteries. The hot rodder in the second rank strips his car of all chromium and ornaments. He lowers the body of the car, often as much as ten inches, to increase roadability and safety. He stresses clean lines, lightness, simplicity, and gasoline economy in his design. He may not change the chassis, but he will surely add disc or hydraulic brakes if needed. He has failed in his avowed objective if the car is poorly constructed, or if it is not safer, better looking, and more efficient than ordinary cars. His car is a pleasure car, and all the changes he makes are practical for everyday road use. If he happens to be interested in competition he is likely to drive against time at the dry lakes outside Los Angeles, or at the various national meets. . . .

What are the cars of the top rank? They are super-streamlined, often made of surplus aircraft wing-tanks, and will run only at top speed. They can be started only if they are pushed, one of the many reasons why they cannot be run on the highway. They are of interest in the hot-rod complex mainly because their owners are the designers and the innovators in the hot-rod field. Many automotive manufacturers, knowing the excellence of the timing apparatus at the lakes, time their own test model there.

Bonneville Salt Flats, Utah, sees hundreds of hot-rodders fussing around trying to gap spark plugs and adjust carburetors in the early mornings of August, at the annual meet. The emphasis there is on speed, power, and streamlining, on a white salt desert that draws hundreds of cars from all over America. This display of engineering skill and aerodynamic ingenuity, however, is only one side of the activity; the idea of selling individualization in body design by rebuilding from originally disparate parts has become a commercial motive of the "body shops." . . .

Rebels with a Cause

There is much evidence that hot-rodding has involved boys of widely varying economic and social backgrounds; and there are indications that it is relaxedly interethnic. The rising costs of hot-rod-car rebuilding may have introduced recent changes, but it is a good guess that hot-rodding still remains in the hands of young men who can plan to spend no more than about $1,200 on a car over a period of three years or so. It is certain that in the 1940's and 1950's the participants in the dry-lake races to some extent engaged in a cross-class conversation, the wide range of classifications, from high-cost to low-cost cars, making that possible. The building of hot-rods calls on the skills of boys who have had some automotive-school training and garage experience, thus tending to draw non-college kids into the field; and many of the hot-rods are built by teams in which there appears to be a division of labor among individuals drawn from different ethnic and social classes as well as from different skill ranks of adolescent society. . . .

The leisure competence of the hot-rodders has been so perceptible in terms of their products and their race meets, as at Bonneville, that one might be tempted to let a favorable case for the fad rest on the excitement that goes with these gasoline fiestas. . . . It seems highly probable that at least some of the sour public responses to the breed, stated in terms of attack upon their lawbreaking, were based on a vaguely sensed envy of the hot-rodder's morale and an even more vaguely felt anxiety about the hot-rodder's satirization of the Detroit car.

The degree to which the hot-rodders have been critical of the commercial-car market in the United States is hard to determine. In the sense that they revolted against the soft-sprung "status car" obligatory for most adults in the American social system, they revolted not so much against the car as against the older generation and its image of the car. On the other hand, if we scan the entire consumer-goods market in the period 1946-56, the scene provides us with no other so deeply felt, widely powerful, and economically penetrating revolution in style organized by the consumers themselves. With every other commodity, in every other market, changes in style have been brought about by research and promotion campaigns; and the public has had its choice of a variety of new products within a broad range of similar style. The hot-rod movement is unique in the history of the market and in the history of "organized" consumers in the last twenty years.

The craftsmanlike revolt that sought technological and artistic integrity and individualization in cars began to change even before 1950, however. The field became more commercialized and respectable; and as it drew greater and greater numbers in, it ceased to be the possession of a passionately different few and became an activity demanding such a high degree of institutional organization that it began to look overorganized. It is possible that the same sort of youth who would have gone into it in 1946 would not go near it today. . . .

Lee Bramson . . . writes:

In California, a new level of competence and organization was introduced around 1950 or so, by the establishment of diplomatic relations between the citizens of the locality and the hot rod club. This was achieved in most cases by a conference with the police officials concerning minimum requirements for the hot rod, which inevitably resulted in some sort of standardization. Also specific areas were made available, as in the case of the dry lakes, where the hot-rodders were allowed free rein. . . . These consolidations imparted a still higher degree of standardization to the hot rod group. . . .

A compelling facet of the hot-rod fad in the United States in the last twenty years or so is its consistently sleazy handling by those parts of the press aimed at readers over the age of eighteen. Newspapers redoubled their criticism of the hot rod precisely during the period when, by holding it down, they could give Detroit time to resist it by partial incorporation. The advertising pages have consistently praised since about 1952 precisely those elements of car design that were attacked in hot rods before that time. Perhaps the only exception is comic-strip-artist Zack Mosley, creator of "Smilin' Jack." . . .

A . . . review of automotive market research (*Fortune*, November 1956) shows that even the most sensitively contrived investigation into the nature of auto sales fails to pick out in advance the trends that will be dominant. This suggests that nothing would be so helpful to styling intelligence in the industry—not to speak of qualitative criticism of design—as small sectors of actual experiment with advance design.

Plainly, the auto companies should make an outright gift of 10 per cent of their capital to the youth of California, who would use it for experimental auto design and construction. On the whole, General Motors might have the most to gain from such a move. If it is an industry with a reputation among the young for sloppy design, its stylistic troubles can probably be arrested by a voluntary surrender of some capital to these very youngsters who hold it in poor repute.

Such a cavalier suggestion, however, no matter how much good it might do the manufacturers, is not the point here. For all its faddishness, hot-rodding deserves study as an attempt to discriminate among the values of an industrial culture. We should be more concerned with the pathos of a social movement among young consumers than with the comedy of a muscle-bound industry.

WATERFRONT AT THE DOORSTEP [4]

Fred Foster lives in the big city—miles from anything resembling a waterway. Yet his smartly styled, bucket-seated boat

[4] From article by W. Clifford Harvey, boating editor, *Christian Science Monitor*. p 9. Je. 15, '63. Reprinted by permission from The Christian Science Monitor. © 1963 The Christian Science Publishing Society. All rights reserved.

is parked in the garage or driveway among the automobiles. What is so unusual about this urban setting—a boat owner and his boat in the center of a canyon of high-rise buildings? Nothing unusual at all, according to the Outboard Marine Corporation of Waukegan, Ill., following a study of the habits of some 40 million participants in recreation on United States waterways. . . . The boat trailer, it seems, has brought the waterfront to the city-family doorstep. The name Fred Foster is fictitious. But the characterization is representative of a new way of family living in which the design of better boat trailers, the building of express highways between city and waterway, and the creation of vast man-made lakes as part of power and flood-control projects have made the urban and suburban dweller boat conscious.

Home yards, garages, and driveways are getting crowded with just about everything that floats and can be trailered over the highways. Or, if they wish, city boat enthusiasts can anchor their crafts in any of the four thousand fully equipped marinas scattered throughout the United States today. Also, there are thousands of additional private and public docking facilities mushrooming in metropolitan regions.

This growth is due to several factors: spectacular prosperity throughout the country, increased leisure time, the national search for relief from traffic-jammed highways, and modern manufacturing techniques and materials that have built volume into boat production and savings into consumer prices.

The rush of Americans to the waterways cannot be laid to any single factor or group of factors. It could be World War II research—if anything—that generated the spectacular techniques advancing the outboard motor to its presently dominating position in boat propulsion.

Only ten years ago, Johnson Motors brought out the first big-horsepowered outboard—the famous "25." In that year, the average horsepower of all outboard motors was 8.9. In 1962, it was 30.3. It was this technique of building big engines that set the pace for the popular boating boom of today.

A recent breakthrough in engines was the quiet motor. Again it was Johnson which introduced the principle of rubber mountings, developed cover cushioning, isolated the powerhead and reduced the irritating howl of the outboard to a mere hum.

From then on, the boating revolution developed into a chain of innovations and popular demands. Reinforced fiberglass was unheard of prior to World War II. Between 1946 and 1953 about four thousand boats were built of this material. But one thing leads to another in boat building and designing. Fiberglass made it possible to vary the shapes of hulls. Out of this flexibility in design came the multiple-hulled boats, the double- and triple-runner catamarans and trimarans.

Research Races Ahead

This year the competition race of research and development moves into the fields of jet propulsion, hydrofoils, inboard-outboard motors, and all-unit-packaged boats or "outboards ready for the water on delivery." The boat, motor, controls, and propeller are all matched in a single packaged unit.

Jet propulsion is new to the marine field. Yet, more than twenty companies are already producing smallcraft "jets" in the United States. The system consists of a water-jet unit driven by either a conventional inboard or outboard engine. These boats require neither propeller or rudder. All that is visible of the propulsion system is a type of sturdy tail-pipe, fitted with deflectors that direct exhaust flow and in so doing steer the boat. They are highly maneuverable and can operate in shallow depths at racing speeds.

The inboard-outboard drive puts the motor inside the boat and the propeller outside in such convenient manner that, if the propeller is damaged, it can be easily repaired. The inboard-outboard is adding to its numbers annually.

For the future, the industry looks to the hydrofoil system of riding above the water, rather than on it. These are conventional, light-weight boats with hydrofoils attached to the bottoms of the hulls. Hydrofoils are similar to small waterwings. As the boat gathers speed, the foils lift the hull completely free of the surface of the water. Result—a bump-free ride. The boats can be powered by inboards or outboards, and the foils are retractable. . . .

"It is the industry consensus," according to the Outboard Boating Club of America, "that major manufacturers of outboard engines are working on gas turbines, even as they are in the automobile field. We believe that you can expect to see hydrofoils become popular for boat hulls in the very near future.". . .

Then there is the Amphicar. It rides equally well along the road or on the water. Developed under the eyes of wartime researchers, the car is driven on land like a conventional automobile. In the water, it gets power thrust from twin screws, with the front wheels acting as rudders. The underbody is sealed tight and the doors are thoroughly waterproofed.

CAMPS FOR CHILDREN [5]

While camping is not a new activity, it is undergoing a re-emphasis as an educational medium. The popularity of school camps, community camps, and day camps is virtually taking the country by storm. This is justly so since camping offers a most interesting and natural setting for the learning process. Moreover, crowded city living, with its emphasis on brick, cement, and steel, has made little provision for nature. Even for the lad who comes from a country setting, the camp offers a most desirable setting for learning to get along with others, practicing the give and take of communal living, and developing self-reliance in the out-of-doors. While not a complete justification for camping, this explanation can at least partially account for its rapid rise in popularity.

In addition, camping can serve as a bromide to the high-strung and complex living of our time. It is an activity that can

[5] From *Recreation Leadership*, 2nd Edition, by H. Dan Corbin, professor of physical health, State Teachers College, Lock Haven, Pennsylvania. p 335-57. © 1959, by permission of Prentice-Hall, Inc., Englewood Cliffs, New Jersey.

be practiced alone as well as with mixed groups, and by family groups regardless of financial standing. The individual, no matter what his age, can discover in camping an interest that will carry over into later life and one that will grow in appreciation along with each experience.

Camping as we know it today owes much of its success and acceptance to the private camp, for it served as the forerunner of our present day camping program. It pioneered by experimenting and conducting varied activities. While there are many camps that simply transfer the physical education program of the school into a setting of trees and grass, this faulty emphasis is fortunately not attributable to all. Most camp leaders recognize that the locale of the camp is unique for acquiring the knowledge and skills of the outdoors with its nature lore, wood crafts, Indian lore, and the like.

The organization that has been instrumental in fostering advancement in camping more than perhaps any other is the American Camping Association. Its membership is countrywide. . . .

Types of Camps

There is an assortment of camps which may be classified according to financial backing. Institutional camps are exemplified by those conducted by the Boy and Girl Scouts, boys' clubs, 4-H clubs, settlement houses, "Y's," church and school camps, among others. They serve a unique purpose in that they make camp available for many who could not otherwise attend the more costly private camps. In addition, there are health camps conducted by service clubs and charitable groups, sportsmen's club camps, public camps run by city, state, and Federal agencies, conservation camps which are concerned with human and natural resource protection, and camps for the atypical such as the crippled, blind, cerebral palsied, and cardiac, whose ailments make it difficult for them to fit into the regular camping activities. These are in addition to the hundreds of private camps which are usually more costly, attendance for an eight-week period usually ranging from $250 to more than twice that amount.

Camping has become a recognized adjunct of the curricula of a growing number of school systems. The importance of this phase was highlighted by the undertaking of the Outdoor Education Project under the sponsorship of the American Association for Health, Physical Education and Recreation and the leadership of Julian W. Smith. He has conducted outdoor education workshops throughout the country. The efforts of such states as Michigan, California, New York, Texas and Pennsylvania have not only helped stimulate programs in their own borders but have exerted desirable influences on neighboring states and regions. A number of colleges have helped spearhead school camping by way of conducting demonstrations, workshops, seminars and the issuance of descriptive literature. . . .

A concern for education in the protection and judicious use of the country's water, minerals, soil, forests and wildlife is advocated in the conservation camp. Field trips and lectures are often used to impart an understanding of the importance of stream pollution, reforestation, farm fish ponds, forest game, land reclamation, and erosion, to our natural resources. . . .

The drift toward community camping, which is unmistakable although still progressing at a slow pace, includes cities like Oakland, California, which recognized the need long ago, and Dearborn, Michigan, whose program is of more recent date. An opportunity to camp at a minimal cost is needed greatly by countless communities. . . .

On January 1, 1948, Dearborn purchased 240 acres of land for . . . [a community camp]. While it was inaugurated as a day camping experience, it became so popular that it was doubled in 1949. Although still predominantly a day camping set-up, overnight camping, family camping, and picnic camping are becoming increasingly popular.

There is a growing need for increased emphasis on family camping. In view of our growing leisure, longer paid vacations, renewed emphasis on togetherness, and the trend toward outdoor living, family camping warrants a more vital position in recreation programing. Although more communities are adopting this program feature, it is still short of the acceptance . . . [it] deserves. . . .

A laboratory situation for the application of skills taught at camp is available in the outpost camp. Skills learned in camp such as axemanship, cooking, nature lore, camp making, outfitting, mapping, and first aid are afforded practice opportunities in a real situation. . . .

Short-term camping refers to day, overnight, and week-end camping. . . . Scouting has for years expounded these virtues and encouraged the practice of short-term camping. . . .

The day camp movement has been gaining in popularity at a very rapid pace. It is being adopted by many city recreation departments and by numerous settlement houses, boys' clubs, and "Y's." Day camps are usually located within a large city park (as in the city of Pittsburgh) or on roof tops (as is the case in many settlement houses and boys' clubs in New York City and elsewhere).

The usual practice is for the camper to be picked up after breakfast, to eat lunch at the camp, and to return in time for his evening meal. Food is often provided by the camp itself. For many youngsters in city areas, this experience offers an opportunity to exchange a tenement house setting for a countrified one with an opportunity to play in a natural setting. . . .

Camp Programs

The camping program should be varied, flexible, and comprehensive. Activities that lend themselves to the camp's natural setting should be emphasized. This is not meant to preclude the use of sports, games, and physical education activities. By virtue of its setting, the unique atmosphere of the camp warrants the stressing of nature lore, camp fire activities, cook-outs, hiking, trail blazing, and ceremonials befitting the camp situation. . . . An overemphasis on games will be the case if such worthwhile activities as handicrafts, dramatics, music, story telling, and varied hobby groups are slighted. A balanced program similar to the one indicated is more apt to leave the participant with a feeling of worthwhile accomplishment. Not only will there be fun in the doing but also gratification from having completed meaningful tasks. . . .

A partial list [of special events] follows with the realization that the imagination of a leader can bring forth others that are perhaps more meaningful to his situation and more in keeping with the interests of his group:

Splash Parties
Socials and Parties
Camp Fire Programs
Story Telling
Camp Sings
Quiz Shows
Forums
Barbecues-Wiener Roasts
Tournaments
Hikes (Short or Overnight)
Explorations
Fishing Trips

Trail Blazing
Axemanship
Knot Tying
Fly Tying
Bait Casting Exhibitions
Marksmanship
Nature Expeditions
Water Pageants
Treasure and Scavenger Hunts
Visitations (Farms, Canneries,
  Water Works, etc.)
Canoe Trips

MUNICIPAL SPORTS FITNESS CAMPS [6]

Every boy and girl needs a balanced program of physical education, health education, and recreation. Therefore, Portland, Oregon, has developed sports-fitness camps as part of its summer youth program. The summer sports camp provides activities that develop strength, flexibility, endurance, and coordination. It provides opportunity to participate in sports and other physical activities and contributes to the wholesome use of leisure, the creation of character, and the development of health and optimum physical fitness. It helps youngsters participate in sports in a sportsman-like manner; to appreciate techniques, strategy, artistry, accomplishment, and similar qualities in the performance of sports; to appreciate the history of sports; to appreciate the cultural

[6] From "Sports Fitness Camps," by Dorothea Graham, sports fitness director, Bureau of Parks and Public Recreation, Portland, Oregon. *Recreation*. 57:280-1. Je. '64. Reprinted by permission.

significance of sports; and to appreciate the personal significance of sports and other physical-education activities.

The sports-fitness camp was established to meet the fitness needs of youth in the city within the program of the Bureau of Parks and Public Recreation. Since its inception seven years ago, it has been one of the most popular activities of the summer. The program has developed from one camp into three. . . . The first camp was situated at a park next to a high school where gym facilities were available. However, to draw interest in the program at that time, the major portion of the program was held out of doors. This involved moving the trampoline, mats, et cetera, but the advertising results were tremendous, and the staff felt that all the hard work was well worth the moving of equipment.

A large portion of the program is still carried on outside, and, with the cooperation of the school district, the camps have full use of the school athletic facilities, particularly the apparatus and wrestling rooms used daily for various activities. Maintenance is carried out by school or park depending upon the facilities used and all equipment is furnished by the park department.

At each of the three camps, enrollment is limited to a maximum of sixty-five boys and the same number of girls. Each child must have reached his ninth birthday before the camp starts and must not be over thirteen. All sessions are usually filled by June 1, with the program starting around the fifteenth of the month.

Each camper registers in advance for a choice of sessions. There are three sessions of three weeks, Monday through Friday. The day is divided, with the girls arriving at 9 A.M., and ending at noon, and the boys participating from 1:30 to 4:30 P.M. There is a small registration fee charged which includes a lettered T-shirt.

The staff is composed of directors particularly interested in sports, who have a general knowledge of all activities, and who are possibly specialists in one particular field. This staff of three, one woman and two men, work with both the girls and boys, and it has been found to balance the program quite well.

One day at the beginning and end of each session is devoted to physical-fitness testing. The six-part test includes sit-ups, pull-ups (modified for girls), shuttle run, standing broad jump, softball throw, and fifty-yard dash. . . . Each child keeps an individual scoresheet and these are filed away and are taken home after the last test. . . .

The campers are divided into one of three groups according to ability and age classification, dependent upon the first-day testing program. These groups participate in three different activities for the next hour and a half on a rotating basis, with a change of staff personnel. Each group picks a name; they have come up with "Hellcats," "Unbeatables," Physical Wrecks," et cetera. The activities may include gymnastics and posture training—apparatus, tumbling, stunts, trampoline, balance beams, and posture training—and sports and games—basic mechanics of individual play and team strategy, including games of simple organization, soccer, volleyball, touch football, softball for girls, wrestling, and tennis.

During the three weeks in track and field, the camper works to attain his AAU Junior Physical Fitness certificate. This has been a keen source of individual competition and has increased the interest in track and field in the area. Not all campers pass the test and receive their awards, but all have tried and worked toward this final achievement. Included in the citywide program is a weekly track meet in which all campers are encouraged to participate.

Apparatus is developing new popularity with the use of rings, bars, springboard, horse, buck, et cetera. Many of the boys and girls have been introduced to this equipment at camp and have been quite amazed at the stunts and various tricks they can accomplish in a short time with the proper teaching techniques. . . .

For the younger camper there is particular stress on basic movements—how to catch, throw and kick a ball (softball, soccer, volleyball, football). By the means of adapted relays and games, these techniques are then put into motion. It is always a source of inspiration to the staff to see the gains made along this line.

The last activity period of the day is devoted to swimming. Instruction follows the teaching progression . . . [of] the American Red Cross, and ARC tests are administered and certificates awarded to those who qualify. Many of the campers are ardent swim enthusiasts and have entered swim meets both in and out of the city. But the great thrill comes when they compete against the other camps in the city during the final week. At times the program is handicapped by the weather as some of the outdoor pools are not heated, but the staff has discovered if it can entice the youngsters in for a strenuous fifteen minutes of instruction they are not so aware of the cold or rainy weather. Dryland swimming in the gymnasium has proven to be satisfactory, particularly on elementary backstroke, buddy rescue, use of life jackets, et cetera. All campers must participate in the life-jacket drill and all nonswimmers are given a lead-up by various methods.

The sports-fitness camp is a program which is enjoying success and points out that discipline can and will be endured by the youngsters during the summer months. They know there are certain rules and regulations that must be adhered to, and yet the fun element plays a very important part in the daily schedule.

TO CAMP OR NOT TO CAMP [7]

In anticipation of the eventual arrival of the summer travel season, this section published on March 12 [1961] an article by Joseph F. Hannan, who reported on a motor-camping trip his family had taken last summer. His article was an attempt to warn other first-time campers who might be struck by the series of natural, automotive and financial catastrophes that pursued his family on their holiday trip. Mr. Hannan's account, titled "It Isn't So What They Say About Camping," struck a spark in the soul of Mrs. Katherine Lynch, who by coincidence also lives in New Jersey, and on March 26 her article, "Another View of

[7] From article in New York *Times*. Section X. p 31+. My. 7, '61. © 1961 by The New York Times Company. Reprinted by permission.

Camping: Family of Six Doubles Its Vacation Costs With a Tent," appeared in this section.

Thereupon the campers of America, with all the vehemence of an organized minority group, which they appear not to be, united to turn their pens and typewriters sharply against Mr. Hannan and Mrs. Lynch. The flow of letters turned into a flood of manuscripts extolling the virtues of camping and decrying those who spurned them, or found life in a tent something less than idyllic.

In the interest of fair play, it must be noted that more of the pro-campers attacked Mrs. Lynch's slightly sorrowful view of camping than set out after Mr. Hannan, and that women campers were more anxious to drive Mrs. Lynch and her family from the campsites than were the male letter writers in defense of the outdoor way of life.

This page has been set aside to air the to-camp-or-not-to-camp debate to its conclusion. . . .

Not all the communications received on both sides of this seemingly controversial subject can be published here. Those that follow have been heavily excerpted.

Run-Through at Home

I could barely contain myself while reading Katherine Lynch's article on camping. Who takes a trip without at least one run-through, at home, of erecting a new tent? Who leaves for any trip without packing first? Who ever heard of setting up camp without looking over the grounds first? Oh lady, please, stay in your beach cottage!

Constance Riesenberg
West Hempstead, N.Y.

Camping Is Fun

I consider myself the hot-house variety of female. I flourish best in the parlor. I like the comforts of home. So, you can imagine it was with great trepidation and much doubting that I let my husband talk me into a camping trip. Both of us are very unathletic, but we are the parents of three sons who are interested in the outdoors.

That first year we rented a camping trailer. We chose a beautiful lakeside campsite in the Adirondacks and we stayed put. Much to my surprise, I enjoyed it. Our youngest was two and a half years old at the time and I had a lot of hand laundering to do.

But the meals were quite simple—how elaborate can you get on a two-burner Coleman stove? Better still, all pitched in and helped. So another family was converted to camping and the great outdoors.

The following year we purchased a station wagon and a tent, air mattresses and sleeping bags. We spent one week at a lake again. However, we were practically old-timers by then, so we set out for Florida that winter.

We spent a rainy but enjoyable two weeks there. Because of the rain and since we were sleeping in the station wagon (we had left the tent at home), we did break the monotony and sleep in motels on three different occasions. We had two bedrooms, living room, kitchen and dining room, bath and screened-in porch for $8.

Last summer, being seasoned campers, we took a 3,500-mile trip to the Gaspé Peninsula, New Brunswick and Nova Scotia in a two-week period. On this trip we slept each night at a campsite, cooked all our meals, took numerous slides and snapshots, and best of all, the total outlay was only $200, including the credit-card charges.

This year we are planning a trip to Yellowstone National Park. We have our maps with routes marked out and are gathering campsite information.

Truly, camping is fun and inexpensive. To us, it is the best way to spend a vacation. We are talking about Mexico next year.

(Mrs.) Jean L. Sherwood
Wayne, N.J.

Practice Makes Perfect

Please tell your readers that any camping trip does take planning. Get all the information you can about the place or places you plan on staying. But first take your family on a trial run, if you have never camped before, preferably over a weekend and close to home. You can't imagine how it helps you see your mistakes and gives you a chance to make the necessary changes before the big trip.

Mrs. Harold D. Keener
Weston, W.Va.

Preparations Count

Camping *can* be fun, in spite of the unhappy views of recent correspondents from New Jersey. People who have really enjoyed camping usually make better preparations than these discouraged souls seem to have done.

A great many people take too much stuff with them when they go camping, some of it so intricate that they cannot use it when they get to a camping area. Not that I would recommend the method we started with, two of us, a number of years ago. We had a pup tent, two sleeping bags, no stove, no tarp, no chairs, no refrigerator, and not even air-mattresses. We believed that those who used air-mattresses were "softies." Maybe so, but we joined the ranks of the air-mattress-users a year or so later.

We camped where fireplaces were provided, and, having no axe, we soon learned to grab the neat kindling other people had cut, just as soon as they vacated their campsites. This is a skill that has stood us in good stead ever since!

What marvelous places we have seen, what wonderful things we have done! And only by camping could we have done them!

Emily F. Ellis
New York, N.Y.

Three Cheers

Three cheers for Katherine Lynch.

During the five years that my family has flirted with the camping mystique, I have not been able to understand what it was that held us back from investing hundreds of dollars and taking to the camping trail. Mrs. Lynch's graphic vignettes have released within me what I now realize were unconscious blocks, a certain foreknowledge that the very catastrophes she describes —if not worse—would befall us.

After reading the article my wife and I looked at each other with the greatest relief and agreed to close the ledger on our camping experience, as yet unborn.

We consider ourselves lucky to have gotten off considerably easier than the Lynches. Total investment in camping equipment (a stove): $14.

Richard Steinman
Ashland, Mass.

A Frightful Picture

Katherine Lynch gives an account of her family's experience with camping, which, if it were anything close to the truth about camping, would be enough to scare the sleeping bag off the back of even such a woodsman as Daniel Boone himself.

Sleeping bags at $40 each? We bought very adequate ones, good to about 10 below freezing, for $16.95 each. A trailer for $150? We use an excellent car-top rack, for $14.95. Six folding chairs for $48? Why drag along folding chairs?

Above all, camping has that most important ingredient of any successful vacation: that in every possible way it should be very different from the way we live the rest of the year.

Jack Grabelsky
Great Neck, N.Y.

Skunks and Rain

Sure, we have had some unnerving experiences, like the night the white skunk came into our tent in search of a cooky our youngest had filed away in his playpen. And the two-week vacation when it rained every single day. But we have had some wonderful experiences, too, ones our family never could have afforded otherwise.

Writing humorously and cynically of camping makes good reading, but thousands of experienced campers (who didn't try to be the Daniel Boone family the first time out) are still going back for more.

Mrs. John B. Scanlan
Emerson, N.J.

MOTEL-HOPPING ACROSS AMERICA [8]

The private automobile still has much to recommend it as a practical mode of transportation for vacationing Americans, particularly those to whom a holiday includes a reasonable degree of comfort and even some pampering. Although costs for such automobile trips have risen since we made our first cross-country trek in 1936—a 3,900-mile, eight-day trip for $122.80—we feel that our recent month-long auto journey was not exorbitant. On some days, we went well over our planned budget of $11 for the car, $11 for food and $10 for accommodations, with $3 earmarked for extras, but there were many days when the total was well under $35.

Travel by automobile is, admittedly, more expensive than by camper, trailer or tramper (a delightful term used by those who load all kinds of sleeping and eating gear into the rear of the family station wagon). However, we wonder if, except for those traveling with several children, the great savings cited are not overemphasized. As for the oft-touted advantage of carrying one's home on one's back and, therefore, being able to camp in areas where restaurants, hotels and motels are nonexistent, we found that traveling in even those areas is possible if one plans in advance and carries a good Thermos.

For us, the principal advantage offered by travel in the family car is the ease of driving a familiar vehicle unencumbered by a camper or trailer, and the comfort we could look forward to at the end of each day's journey. We like our hot tub and shower,

[8] From "Motel-Hopping Across U.S.," by Eunice T. Juckett, travel writer. New York Times. Section X. p 7. S. 13, '64. © 1964 by The New York Times Company. Reprinted by permission.

a good supply of ice in the cooler, and a comfortable bed ready and waiting for us. We also like a good strong light to read by at night, the possibility of watching a favorite television program and perhaps enjoying a swim.

The prospect of eating a well-prepared meal in pleasant surroundings, with no effort on our part, we find important to our vacation. . . . Eating local foods is another joy. . . . We like to sample delights such as boysenberry pie in the Pacific Northwest, baked Idaho potatoes in the heart of south Idaho and the infinite variety of Wisconsin cheeses.

Our camper, tramper and trailer friends tell us we miss the sociability of talking with others at campsites. Perhaps—yet, we have never found any lack of friendliness among fellow motel vacationists.

Because we like to stop over if something interests us, our daily mileages varied considerably. . . . We were thankful that we had only a standard automobile to maneuver around the sharp, unguarded turns and up and down the steep grades of the Far West. Also, parking was never a problem for a car without a trailer.

We carried a minimum of luggage on our thirty-day trip. Our gallon vacuum bottle, two overnight bags and a typewriter fitted on the floor directly behind the front seat. Cameras, film, binoculars and an airline attaché case of maps and travel folders rode the rear seat. Other travel material was always handy in the glove compartment. Our golf bags and large case for extra clothing shared the trunk with the spare tire.

Before we started, we made only one reservation—for the first night in mid-Pennsylvania. This was done because we started at midday and wanted to drive until dark. After the first day, we tried to stop by the middle of the afternoon in order to avoid the "No Vacancy" dilemma, and also to have time for a leisurely drive around the community where we were staying. . . .

Our trip was not just a succession of one-night stands. We spent two nights in Burley, Idaho, where we found a motel with a nine-hole golf course. This stop gave us ample time to visit the world's largest trout farm in nearby Buhl, to go through a giant potato processing plant, and to drive out to the new national monument, the City of Rocks. There, a century ago, Oregon Trail travelers inscribed their names on the weirdly eroded boulders. We also spent five nights in Boise so that we could see some of the fascinating ghost towns in the surrounding country and enjoy the annual Basque Festival. We stopped for four days at Sun Valley, and stayed over at Coeur d'Alene to inspect wartime Camp Farragut, which will be the site of the 1965 Girl Scout Round-Up.

Motel costs varied widely from area to area. The lowest rate we paid was $6; the highest, $13. Total expenses for overnight accommodations came to $261.92. The over-all cost of our 7,941-mile trip was $974.88. . . . This works out to an average daily cost of $32.49. To campers, this may seem like a high price, but we feel our vacation trip was worth every penny. We relaxed, we were waited on, and we have enough memories of striking natural beauty to more than fill dreary winter days.

CONSERVATION IS EVERYBODY'S BATTLE [9]

Not far from where I live in Westchester County, just an hour's drive up the Hudson River from New York City, there is a lovely wild tidal marsh called George's Island. Here the warm breeze brushing past you from the water bobs the cattails and brings the raucous *kong-ker-eeee!* of the redwings that flash among the reeds. There are raccoon and muskrat and possum here, and ornithologists say it is one of the few places in the area where you can spot an alder fly-catcher. The city seems a thousand miles away.

But the true wonder of George's Island is that it exists at all. In 1954 the Federal Government, which owned the marshland, put it up for sale and received a $15,000 bid from a housing developer. Town officials were delighted to have the "useless"

[9] From article by James Nathan Miller, publicist and contributor to national magazines. The article is abridged from "To Save the Landscape." *National Civic Review.* 53:354-9+. Jl. '64. *Reader's Digest.* 85:161-6+. Ag. '64. Reprinted by permission.

marsh filled in and added to the tax rolls, and local merchants welcomed the prospect of more business. Like so many similar plots of meadow and woodland, the poor old swamp had no influential friends—except one determined woman.

Ruth Rusch, a nature writer and conservation chairman of the Ossining Women's Club, rallied a group of like-minded people, waged a four-year battle of committee meetings, letters, petitions and referendums. Along the way she picked up the assistance of Richard Pough, president of the Natural Area Council, a dedicated landsaver who devotes full time to preserving examples of our original landscape. With Pough hitting the higher levels and Mrs. Rusch working the grass roots, their campaign reached every echelon of government. In the end—just as the auctioneer's hammer was poised to knock the swamp down to the builder—the County Park Commission rushed in from the wings and whisked it away. Today the tide pours in and out of the little inlet with the glorious promise that it will do so forever.

The war waged by Ruth Rusch in her little corner of suburbia contains immense significance for all of us. For it shows not only that we can win the fight to save our landscape, but also specifically *how* to go about it.

Disappearing Land

First of all, conservation is no longer a distant, rural concern. It has become a pressing *suburban* problem. In the words of conservationist William H. Whyte, Jr., "The fact that there will remain thousands of acres of empty land in Wyoming is not going to help the man living in Teaneck, New Jersey."

The typical suburban community is threatened by a two-way invasion: as the city reaches out along the main roads, swallowing trout streams, golf courses and woodlands, it is met by the inward rush of new highways and power lines. Land disappears fast. A modern freeway wipes out the equivalent of a fifty-acre park with every mile, a power line more than thirty acres per mile, a jet airport hundreds of acres. This is happening from coast to coast. In Massachusetts, traffic engineers are planning to plaster a highway over the old sloping greensward that has long graced the meandering banks of the Charles River in Cambridge. In California, there are plans for aiming a high-voltage power line smack through the beautiful residential community of Woodside.

Frequently problems pop up almost overnight. In 1957, Massachusetts' Middlesex County decided to develop a beach on Thoreau's beautiful Walden Pond. No advance announcement was made; the crews simply arrived one morning, sawed through two hundred full-grown oaks and pines, then bulldozed tons of forest humus and topsoil into the water to improve the beach. The deed was done in two days; the protests came afterward.

Repelling the Invaders

The only way to stem such invasion is locally and on an emergency basis. . . . During the George's Island fight, Mrs. Rusch too often had to cope with the need for overnight action. So when the battle was over she invited six friends to her house and founded the Emergency Conservation Committee for Westchester and Putnam counties. Serving as a coordinating and information-gathering central headquarters, this committee helped set up local conservation groups that now are constantly ready to move fast as problems come up.

Last winter when the Putnam County-owned Manitou Marsh was threatened by sale to a builder, the committee mobilized its troops with such effect that one town supervisor later said the pressure was the most intense he'd ever experienced. The marsh was saved.

Not long ago, the Peekskill committee heard that a fourteen-acre tract of underdeveloped private land had been offered to the city as a park, but that a resolution was being readied rejecting the offer because it would take the land off the tax rolls. The resolution would be passed at the city-council meeting in two days. Forewarned, the conservation people descended on the meeting to insist that the city accept the park. The resolution was never even read, and today the fourteen acres, known as

Tompkins Park, make a lovely little spot of dappled green with rustic paths and a tumbling brook.

To fight the professional despoilers, you must learn the basic facts and figures of the conservation argument. The housing people, the highway, power-line and airport interests have moved through hundreds of communities; they have lawyers and researchers and public-relations men to present the strongest possible arguments for *their* version of what to do with the land. Too often the only opposition they meet is a band of hastily mobilized housewives and landowners, determined to protect their community but unequipped to debate the fine points. In fact, one of the favorite town-meeting tactics of the developers is to challenge the opposition to debate: they know they can grind opposing arguments to mincemeat.

Here are the two points most frequently raised in such a debate.

The "get-it-on-the-tax-rolls" argument. It goes like this: a park pays no taxes, while the same land in private hands does. Therefore, existing parks are a costly luxury, new ones a wild-eyed extravagance. The fact is that many parks, by increasing the value of the "influenced" land around them, actually produce *more* total taxes than they wipe off the books. A century ago, when New York's Central Park was set aside, the value of the adjoining real estate multiplied eightfold in fifteen years, while the rest of the land in the city merely doubled in worth. . . .

The "economic progress" argument. Generally, the forces most active in trying to fill a community with people beyond its capacity are the builders. Their point of view was well summed up last October [1963] in a statement by a group representing 750 Westchester homebuilding and supply concerns. Attacking the "fanatical" resistance of local governments, they claimed that "obstructionist policies" were keeping the county behind the rest of the country in building progress, blocking fifteen million dollars' worth of construction and causing the loss of 270,000 man-hours of carpentry labor in 1963.

There are two answers to such attacks. First, point to the community in your area where such "economic progress" has reached its zenith. Long Island's Nassau County, smothered by hundreds of square miles of housing developments, is the classic example of the kind of "progress" that results when no "obstructionist policies" inhibit the builders' dreams. Second, answer them on their own ground of economic advantage. In the long run it is the decently preserved communities that will attract the kind of business that makes for truly healthy growth. In explaining why the Prudential Insurance Company selected Boston for a new regional headquarters, a spokesman said, "With each new office we have had to face the problem of transferring key employees. One of the motivating forces that attracts people to one place over another is the availability of attractive recreation outlets."

One valuable aid in blocking would-be despoilers is the "conservation inventory." Find out how nature zoned your area, dividing it into swampland, woods, etc. Then determine how much of this natural zoning remains, and what parts should be put beyond reach of further encroachment. Here are some points that will put your inventory in terms that will be remembered.

Show what's happened to the water table. When Mrs. Rusch checked in 1957, she found that well-drillers were reaching down an average of 160 feet for water, as opposed to only 90 feet in 1937. The reason is obvious: when swamps are drained or brooks channeled in concrete conduits, or trees and topsoil scalped off the land and replaced with buildings and paving, the earth loses its blotter action and the water runs off.

Get firsthand descriptions and pictures of past floods in the area. Brooks and creeks may go for years without overflowing their banks, and their natural flood plains may be covered with houses. When floods come, property damage is then added devastatingly to the havoc.

Be alert to complaints of muddy streams, muddy roads, muddy swimming pools. Mud means erosion, in many cases caused by land-scalping. In Union County, New Jersey, the park commission has spent $20,000 since 1953 removing silt and debris from

Echo Lake, all because developers stripped the vegetation off the lake's upland drainage area.

Most important, focus attention on the worst examples of urban sprawl in your area. Emphasize the fact that the kind of saturation typified by Nassau County can be avoided by maintaining ten to twelve acres of open space per one thousand population.

Strategy for Battle

Know the specific laws and tactics that are available to you and your local government for getting action. There are more than most people realize.

Publicity. This is perhaps the basic weapon, for conservationists almost invariably find that the vast majority of the people are on their side but are unaware of the threatened damage. A conservation committee will receive far more publicity than an individual, since newspapers more readily accept statements from an official body. Mail snapshots to the papers with captions describing the tree about to be knocked down or the stream threatened by a proposed housing development.

Local ordinances. Many towns have passed excellent codes covering the conservation aspects of building. Use them as models. Dover, Massachusetts, has a first-rate ordinance regulating flood-plain building; Summit, New Jersey, has a code preventing indiscriminate tree-cutting in new developments; the town of Cortlandt, New York, has strict regulations governing the removal of topsoil.

Tax-delinquency sales. Often the land least suitable for building—cliffs, gorges, swamps—is the best for conservation purposes, and it is such land that frequently falls into the hands of local governments for nonpayment of taxes. Check the town-hall records to see what is thus available. Your conservation organization may be able to buy it for a few dollars. Recently the Cortlandt conservation group picked up a nice little 125-foot stretch of unspoiled ravine that runs through the village of Croton-on-Hudson: total cost, one dollar.

Acquisition. Most local governments have authority to prevent destruction of good land by acquiring it for parks or recreation purposes. If your local government isn't making use of this power, find out why.

Conservation easements. It is not necessary to *own* property to protect it. Title can be acquired to a certain use of the land—i.e., for its scenic value—thus freezing it in its present state for as long as the easement is held. Such purchases may be too costly in rapidly developing communities, where most owners want to hold the option of eventual sale to developers, but it can be extremely cheap and effective in the long-range protection of rural areas.

Land gifts. Wealthy landowners can actually save money on property or estate taxes by donating land for conservation purposes, while at the same time assuring the enjoyment of it for themselves and their heirs. The Massachusetts Association of Conservation Commissions has published a manual showing simple conservation bequests and deed forms.

Help from outside. A remarkable organization in Washington, D.C., can provide both advice and financial help in saving wilderness tracts of special natural value. Called Nature Conservancy, Inc., it has helped rescue more than one hundred such acres. In some cases it actually takes title to the land; in others, it makes emergency loans to approved conservation groups.

It is an increasingly tough battle to preserve the beauty and dignity of the land we inhabit. But progress is being made and there are enormous satisfactions. Foremost is the discovery, once the battle is joined, that most people are behind you. For there has been a great change in attitudes toward the problem. Looking back at the conservation movements of the Theodore and Franklin Roosevelt eras, President Kennedy called what we're now going through the "third wave."

READING BOOM: BOOKS AND MAGAZINES [10]

A phenomenal rise in sales of books and in the circulation of magazines is making it increasingly difficult to contend, as used frequently to be done, that the United States is becoming a nation of nonreaders. The current boom in books for juveniles likewise seems to expose the needlessness of worrying over whether children are being taught to read. Even television, repeatedly deplored as the thief of reading time for young and old alike, is proving in some cases to act as a spur to reading.

Book sales have been going up steadily for a decade, putting book publishing into the big business category and boosting the value of shares of publishing corporations traded on stock exchanges. On the other hand, growth of the book-buying public has been accompanied by a threat to the retail bookstore in the form of stiff competition from discount sellers. Efforts to adjust to changed conditions in the book market may alter many aspects of book buying and selling.

In a different way, mass readership of the magazines has created problems for their publishers, the chief of which is meeting the costs of large circulations while losing advertising revenue to television. But while the mass-circulation periodicals are having troubles of various kinds, numerous new special-interest journals are entering the field to satisfy the American public's apparently limitless appetite for printed matter.

Increases in Spending for Books

Dollar sales of books in 1960 were 13 per cent ahead of sales in 1959 and approximately double the sales of 1955. Last year's [1960] gain was the largest ever recorded. . . . Americans spent $1.1 billion for books in 1960; they bought some 813 million of them or more than four books each. [It was estimated that book sales totaled over $1.8 billion in 1964.—Ed.]

[10] From pamphlet by Helen B. Shaffer, staff writer, *Editorial Research Reports*. *Editorial Research Reports*. 2, no 23:917-34. D. 20, '61. Reprinted by permission.

Paperback Editions

President Alva H. Parr of the American Booksellers Association . . . told an A.B.A. meeting [June 1961] that a major part of the growth in sales was due to the paperback. The so-called "paperback revolution" is said to date from 1939, when Pocket Books issued its first series of ten reprint titles, to retail at 25 cents and distributed them for sale on newsstands, in drugstores and at other unaccustomed outlets. Within eight years, Pocket Books had sold 200 million copies of 475 titles, and other publishers had successfully entered the field. Although the price of the mass-circulated paperback has risen to 35-75 cents, this type of book is now selling at a rate of nearly a million copies a day.

A second "paperback revolution" started a half-dozen years ago when the so-called "quality paperback" began to appear in quantity. These are books, new titles and reprints, aimed at a more educated or education-seeking buyer, which sell from 95 cents to $2.95. Quality paperback titles include the classics, works of scholarship, anthologies, works on art, music, science, and sociology, and books closely related to courses of study in higher education. A large percentage are nonfiction.

Publishing houses that formerly had no interest in paperbacks, except for sale of the reprint rights to others, have begun to issue their own lines of quality paperbacks. It has been reported that around twenty new paperback publishers have entered the business within the past few years. The Columbia University summer library exhibit last July was devoted solely to quality paperbacks, displaying four thousand titles issued by seventy-two different publishers.

While only a few book stores bothered with paperbacks a few years ago, today few fail to stock a sizable assortment and a number of new stores deal exclusively or primarily in paperbacks. . . . Although profit margins are lower on paperbacks than on hardbacks, the volume of sales they attain and the small amount of store space they require make them a profitable line. A Cincinnati bookstore manages to crowd seven thousand paperbacks into only four hundred square feet of space and the section does an annual business of $50,000.

Magazines

Considerable attention has been directed recently to the financial difficulties of certain mass-circulation magazines. Among magazines thought to be in trouble are some regularly bought by millions of readers. The circulation of the *Saturday Evening Post* had risen to 6.3 million before it carried out, . . . this year [1961], an extensive revision of format designed to improve its financial position. [In 1965 the *Saturday Evening Post* reduced the number of its issues from forty-five to twenty-six.—Ed.] *Coronet* had a circulation of 2.3 million when it published its final issue last October. The main difficulty seems to be that, in the presence of television as a powerful competitor, a large magazine circulation is no longer a sure magnet for advertising. And without a big volume of advertising, a large circulation becomes burdensome to a magazine's publishers.

Termination of a magazine does not reduce the ranks of readers; it merely diverts a group of readers to other periodicals or makes way for new publications. Magazine readership in the United States has been strong for many years and is continuing to rise. A Magazine Advertising Bureau study in 1947 indicated that nearly seven of every ten Americans aged fifteen or over were magazine readers, and that the average reader kept up with four or five periodicals. There is every reason to believe that the percentage of magazine readers is even higher today. *Reader's Digest,* which attained a circulation of 12 million last year, is . . . guaranteeing advertisers 13.3 million by January 1962. *Mc-Call's,* which had 5.7 million readers two years ago, expected to sell 8 million copies of its December issue. Other mass-circulation magazines are experiencing similar growth of readership.

The aggregate circulation of the 120 most popular magazines now averages out to approximately one copy per issue for every individual in the United States. At least forty-five magazines have circulations of a million or more. But the mass-circulation magazines do not give the full picture of magazine reading today. There are approximately seven thousand periodicals, including not only the widely known magazines but also professional, trade, sports, juvenile, school and organization journals, house organs and other publications.

The *Columbia Journalism Review,* itself a new magazine, noted in its initial Fall 1961 issue that the circulation boom had extended not only to mass-readership periodicals but also to the so-called "thinking magazines," which are not designed to attract a mass readership. The *Review* quoted an advertising executive as reporting that the "total gross circulations of so-called thought leader magazines, *Atlantic, Harper's, The Reporter, Saturday Review,* and *Fortune,* have shown a rise of 87 per cent over 1950 and 250 per cent over 1940." On the other hand, the circulation of leading confession magazines—appealing primarily to people with relatively little schooling—had increased only 40 per cent. "The circulation of *True Story* is ten times that of *Saturday Review,* but in 1940 *True Story* had seventy times the circulation of *Saturday Review.*"

The New Republic experienced a 76 per cent increase in circulation from 1959 to 1960. *The Reporter's* circulation rose eightfold in ten years. The *Saturday Review,* emphasizing literary criticism and other fare for cultivated tastes, had a circulation in 1960 of a quarter of a million; the circulation of *Harper's* was slightly higher, that of the *Atlantic* was 260,000, and that of *The New Yorker* was nearly half a million.

At least twenty new magazines have been launched this year, most of them aimed at a specialized rather than a mass readership. Some are hobby magazines, some are for travel enthusiasts, a number make a serious effort to inform the reader or guide his understanding of world problems. . . .

Pamphlets and Government Publications

Books and magazines do not comprise the sole media of popular reading. Newspapers are not only a staple for the dissemination of news; they have come more and more to offer features similar to those appearing in magazines. The syndicated magazine sections of Sunday papers command a readership more than twice that of the most popular of all periodicals.

In addition, innumerable pamphlets of specialized interest are issued by universities and colleges, foundations, business, professional and civic organizations and other agencies. The Federal Government alone makes a formidable contribution to this wealth of reading matter. The report of the Government Printing Office for the fiscal year 1961 showed an inventory of 25,900 active titles. In the year ended last June 30 [1960], more than 53 million copies of government publications were sold, up from 49.5 million in 1959. . . .

Book Clubs and Public Libraries

Books had no such economic prop [as advertising]; they thrived only on receipts from sales. New merchandising techniques, however, helped to promote a wide readership, particularly for a limited number of best sellers. Book clubs, dating from launching of the Book-of-the-Month Club in 1926, gave publishers an assured market for certain titles and usually stimulated the general sale of a book. The paperback revolution and the marketing of books through mass-distribution systems, providing retail outlets in drugstores, supermarkets, newsstands and the like, increased the number of book readers still more.

Growth of libraries offers another index to the readership proclivities of the population. The importance of the library in supplying the demand for reading was demonstrated during the early years of the Great Depression, when most people had little spending power. Between 1929 and 1933, the circulation of books in public libraries rose by nearly 40 per cent and 4 million persons were added to the number of library-card holders.

The most recent statistics on public library use show that in the decade of the 1950's, the number of books circulated increased again by around 40 per cent, which was about twice the rate of increase of the number of books on the shelves. Government surveys of public library systems in cities of more than 50,000 population showed a per capita circulation of approximately five books in the year ended June 30, 1959. During the decade, an increasing percentage of the books circulated were juveniles; surveys in cities with a population of 100,000 to one million showed that more books for juveniles than for adults were circulated, while elsewhere the reverse was true.

Librarians are now worried lest their facilities be swamped by the growing student population. Shortages of trained personnel and of funds to acquire new books and other materials cause special concern. The Library Services Act of 1956 provided funds for expansion of library facilities in underserviced areas of the country, particularly rural sections. (The original five-year life of the Library Services Act was extended by Congress this year for another five years.) Federal aid has made possible the establishment of libraries in 169 cities and townships which formerly had none and for the addition of two hundred bookmobiles to rural library routes. By last June 30, the new facilities had given access to libraries for the first time to an estimated 4 million persons and had improved facilities for 32 million more.

The Actual Extent of Reading

Despite all these indications of a vast consumption of printed matter, the cry is continually raised that only a small and shrinking proportion of the population reads books. Increasing emphasis on audiovisual methods of teaching has aroused fear that the reading habit is not being inculcated into the youth of the nation. Some go so far as to predict that the dominance of books in disseminating knowledge is on the decline.

The *American Library and Book Trade Annual, 1961* says that "The best available studies of the prevalence of book reading in the United States suggest that even by the most optimistic standard, the average is not what it should be." A college president recently said it could not be asserted "that large numbers of students . . . are constantly and eagerly clutching books in their hot little hands," for "most of them aren't." He quoted a Harvard English professor to the effect that "Most students entering college today have read little literature, know almost nothing of the classics."

A Gallup poll in April 1959 found that only 21 per cent of adults questioned had read a book within the month. A poll nine years earlier had given the same result, putting the United States sixth in rank after England, 55 per cent; Norway, 43 per cent; Canada, 40 per cent; Australia, 35 per cent and Sweden, 33 per cent. A new book on Soviet education by an American professor [*What Ivan Knows that Tommy Doesn't* (1961), by Arthur S. Trace, Jr.] asserts that the Russians do a better job than Americans in teaching children to read, and that they do more to inculcate a love for good reading. Like many criticisms of reading habits in this country, the complaint is not that Americans don't read but that too much of their reading is not worth while.

Some would describe as readers only those who regularly read serious books, books of literary merit, or periodicals which demand a certain degree of intellectual effort. Obviously most reading is not of this kind. Some books that push up the sales curve are scarcely books in a real sense at all. The term "nonbook" has been coined to describe volumes of cartoons or pictures, puzzle books, cook books and the like.

Need to Encourage Reading

The big question is whether Americans in the future will go on reading for pleasure or whether other media of entertainment will prove more attractive. Much of the book boom is attributable to rising sales of books for students, chiefly textbooks and quality paperbacks. No one can say whether these "captive readers" will continue to be book readers after their formal education is completed. On the other hand, growth of school libraries and paperback stores in schools and colleges and the mushrooming of junior book clubs and book fairs may help to establish permanent reading habits.

Movies, radio, and television were viewed in turn by book-lovers as enemies. Yet these media have at times served greatly to stimulate the reading of books. Some publishers now "tie in" book advertising with stage, screen or TV productions. Some programs are specifically designed to encourage reading. Westinghouse Broadcasting Company has prepared a series of programs designed to encourage use of public libraries by children aged 6-12. The programs, offered free to television stations across the country, feature narration and animated illustrations of children's classics.

Availability of good literature and scholarly works in paper-backs makes it possible for teachers to assign more outside reading and require more independent research. General Electric Foundation has financed the free distribution of two thousand paperbacks to upperclassmen in the Engineering College of the University of Cincinnati "to encourage the student to form lasting habits of planned reading." The books are not on engineering but include works of fiction, drama, poetry, philosophy, religion, history, psychology, education, fine arts and the natural sciences. If the program is well received, it will be extended to other departments of the university. Another hopeful sign for the future is that for the first time a large apartment development in New York City is to include a free library among its community facilities.

Effects on Book Industry

The boom in book sales has not only brought unprecedented prosperity to the book industry; it has also led to changes in book publishing and selling. Publishing used to be a highly personal enterprise, carried on by an individual imbued with a love of books. The typical publishing house was a partnership or family business. Within the past few years, however, a number of well-known publishers have offered shares to the public. And various publishing houses have merged to form large corporations whose stock is listed on the New York Stock Exchange. The result may be, it is feared, to shift emphasis from quality to quantity, from books for their own sake to books for the profit they may bring.

One of the major influences on modern book publishing is the dominance of the best seller in economics of the industry. The rise of book clubs played a large part in expanding the market, but for only a few titles. The success of the clubs drove home to publishers the possibility of enlarging profits by concentrating promotional efforts on a few books with exceptional sales prospects—regardless of what else they published. Advertising of books tended to be centered on books selected by the clubs or books which otherwise showed signs of becoming money-makers. The clubs and the best-seller concept introduced a new competitive element in book publishing, as each publisher vied for what he hoped would be a best-seller title.

Rising costs of book production made it all the more important that works chosen for publication attract a large public. It was no longer possible to run a publishing house profitably with a wide variety of titles, most of which had only a modest sale that might or might not continue over a period of years. It seemed better to restrict the general list and try to strike gold with a few books that seemed to have best-seller potentialities. After more than forty years in publishing, Alfred A. Knopf mourned the passing of the old days:

> It was a good business in those days. . . . Publishers knew what they wanted . . . and authors supplied it.
>
> Then new publishers began to appear, competition for publishable books became keener, costs increased steadily, and the spread between the sales of the average book and the best seller grew greater. Book clubs appeared with their large cash guarantees for a few titles each year. . . . And so it becomes more and more difficult to get a reasonable hearing for a book that is simply good—not a world-shaking masterpiece, not the choice of a major book club, not to be made into a supercolossal movie, but just a good book in which its publisher and author both believe and which several thousand Americans would probably read with pleasure and profit.

Since Knopf wrote these words, the trend toward big business in publishing has continued. The desire to raise capital to modernize the production and distribution of a mass-market product accounts largely for the trend away from individual or family ownership of publishing houses. [Knopf's company was acquired by Random House in 1960.—Ed.] The healthy demand for books has made it possible to attract the capital of investors who had never thought of putting money into so risky an enterprise.

A SAD HEART AT THE SUPERMARKET [11]

Advertising men, businessmen, speak continually of "media" or "the media" or "the mass media"—one of their trade journals is named, simply, *Media*. It is an impressive word: one imagines Mephistopheles offering Faust media that no man has ever known. . . . The word, like others, has the clear fatal ring of that new world whose space we occupy so luxuriously and precariously; the world that produces mink stoles, rockabilly records, and tactical nuclear weapons by the million; the world that Attila, Galileo, Hansel and Gretel never knew.

And yet, it's only the plural of "medium." "Medium," says the dictionary, "that which lies in the middle; hence, middle condition or degree. . . . A substance through which a force acts or an effect is transmitted. . . . That through or by which anything is accomplished; as, an advertising *medium*. . . . *Biol.* A nutritive mixture or substance, as broth, gelatin, agar, for cultivating bacteria, fungi, etc." Let us name *our* trade journal *The Medium*. For all these media (television, radio, movies, popular magazines, and the rest) are a single medium, in whose depths we are all being cultivated. This medium is of middle condition or degree, mediocre; it lies in the middle of everything, between a man and his neighbor, his wife, his child, his self; it, more than anything else, is the substance through which the forces of our society act upon us, make us into what our society needs.

And what does it need? For us to need . . . Oh, it needs for us to do or be many things—to be workers, technicians, executives, soldiers, housewives. But first of all, last of all, it needs for us to be buyers; consumers; beings who want much and will want more—who want consistently and insatiably. Find some spell to

[11] From article by Randall Jarrell, poet, critic, and professor of English, Woman's College, University of North Carolina. *Daedalus.* 89:357-72. Spr. '60. Reprinted by permission.

make us no longer want the stoles, the records, and the weapons, and our world will change into something to us unimaginable. Find some spell to make us realize that the product or service which seemed yesterday an unthinkable luxury is today an inexorable necessity, and our world will go on. It is the Medium which casts this spell—which is this spell. As we look at the television set, listen to the radio, read the magazines, the frontier of necessity is always being pushed forward. The Medium shows us what our new needs are—how often, without it, we should not have known!—and it shows us how they can be satisfied: they can be satisfied by buying something. The act of buying something is at the root of our world: if anyone wishes to paint the beginning of things in our society, he will paint a picture of God holding out to Adam a checkbook or credit card or Charga-Plate. . . .

Children of three or four can ask for a brand of cereal, sing some soap's commercial; by the time that they are twelve they are not children but teen-age consumers, interviewed, graphed, analyzed. They are on their way to becoming that ideal figure of our culture, the knowledgeable consumer. I'll define him: the knowledgeable consumer is someone who, when he goes to Weimar, knows how to buy a Weimaraner. He has learned to understand life as a series of choices among the things and services of this world; because of being an executive, or executive's wife, or performer, or celebrity, or someone who has inherited money, he is able to afford the choices that he makes, with knowing familiarity, among restaurants, resorts, clothes, cars, liners, hits or best-sellers of every kind. We may still go to Methodist or Baptist or Presbyterian churches on Sunday, but the Protestant ethic of frugal industry, of production for its own sake, is gone. Production has come to seem to our society not much more than a condition prior to consumption: "The challenge of today," writes a great advertising agency, "is to make the consumer raise his level of demand." This challenge has been met: the Medium has found it easy to make its people feel the continually increasing lacks, the many specialized dissatisfactions (merging into one great dissatisfaction, temporarily assuaged by new purchases) that it needs for them to feel. . . . It is a standard joke of our culture that when a woman is bored or sad she buys something to make herself feel better; but in this respect we are all women together, and can hear complacently the reminder of how feminine this consumer-world of ours is. . . .

Our society has delivered us—most of us—from the bonds of necessity, so that we no longer need worry about having food enough to keep from starving, clothing and shelter enough to keep from freezing; yet if the ends for which we work, of which we dream, are restaurants and clothes and houses, consumption, possessions, how have we escaped? We have merely exchanged man's old bondage for a new voluntary one. But *voluntary* is wrong: the consumer is trained for his job of consuming as the factory worker is trained for his job of producing; and the first is a longer, more complicated training, since it is easier to teach a man to handle a tool, to read a dial, than it is to teach him to ask, always, for a name-brand aspirin. . . .

Emerson, in his spare stony New England, a few miles from Walden, could write:

> Things are in the saddle
> And ride mankind.

He could say more now: that they are in the theater and studio, and entertain mankind; are in the pulpit and preach to mankind. The values of business, in an overwhelmingly successful business society like our own, are reflected in every sphere: values which agree with them are reinforced, values which disagree are canceled out or have lip-service paid to them. In business what sells is good, and that's the end of it—that is what *good* means. . . .

The values of the Medium (which is both a popular business itself and the cause of popularity in other businesses) are business values: money, success, celebrity. If we are representative members of our society, the Medium's values are ours; even when we are unrepresentative, nonconforming, our hands are (too often) subdued to the element they work in, and our unconscious expectations are all that we consciously reject. (Darwin said that he always immediately wrote down evidence against a theory because otherwise, he'd noticed, he would forget it; in the same way we keep forgetting the existence of those poor and unknown failures whom we might rebelliously love and admire.) *If you're so smart why aren't you rich?* is the ground-bass of our society, a grumbling and quite unanswerable criticism, since the society's nonmonetary values *are* directly convertible into money. (Celebrity turns into testimonials, lectures, directorships, presidencies, the capital gains of an autobiography *Told To* some professional ghost who photographs the man's life as Bachrach photographs his body.) When Liberace said that his critics' unfavorable reviews hurt him so much that he cried all the way to the bank, one had to admire the correctness and penetration of his press-agent's wit: in another age, what mightn't such a man have become!

Our culture is essentially periodical: we believe that all that is deserves to perish and to have something else put in its place. We speak of "planned obsolescence," but it is more than planned, it is felt—is an assumption about the nature of the world. The present is better and more interesting, more real, than the past; the future will be better and more interesting, more real, than the present. (But, consciously, we do not hold against the present its prospective obsolescence.) Our standards have become, to an astonishing degree, those of what is called "the world of fashion," where mere timeliness—being orange in orange's year, violet in violet's—is the value to which all other values are reducible. In our society "old-fashioned" is so final a condemnation that a man like Norman Vincent Peale can say about atheism or agnosticism simply that it is old-fashioned; . . .

All this is, at bottom, the opposite of the world of the arts, where commercial and scientific progress do not exist; where the bone of Homer and Mozart and Donatello is there, always, under the mere blush of fashion; where the past—the remote past, even—is responsible for the way that we understand, value, and act in, the present. . . . An artist's work and life presuppose continuing standards, values stretched out over centuries or millennia, a future that is the continuation and modification of the past, not its contradiction or irrelevant replacement. He is working for the time that wants the best that he can do: the present, he hopes—but if not that, the future. . . .

In the past our culture's frame of reference, its body of common knowledge (its possibility of comprehensible allusion) changed slowly and superficially; the amount added to it or taken away from it in any ten years was a small proportion of the whole. Now in any ten years a surprisingly large proportion of the whole is replaced. Most of the information people have in common is something that four or five years from now they will not even remember having known. . . . Songs disappear in two or three months, celebrities in two or three years; most of the Medium is lightly felt and soon forgotten. What is as dead as day-before-yesterday's newspaper, the next-to-the-last number on the roulette wheel? and most of the knowledge we have in common is knowledge of such newspapers, such numbers. But the novelist or poet or dramatist, when he moves a great audience, depends upon the deep feelings, the live unforgotten knowledge, that the people of his culture share; if these have become contingent, superficial, ephemeral, it is disastrous for him.

New products and fashions replace the old, and the fact that they replace them is proof enough of their superiority. Similarly, the Medium does not need to show that the subjects that fill it are timely or interesting or important—the fact that they are its subjects makes them so. . . .

After driving for four or five minutes along the road outside my door, I come to a long row of one-room shacks about the size of kitchens, made out of used boards, metal signs, old tin roofs. To the people who live in them an electric dishwasher of one's own is as much a fantasy as an ocean liner of one's own. But since the Medium (and those whose thought is molded by it) does not perceive them, these people are themselves a fantasy: no matter how many millions of such exceptions to the general rule there are, they do not really exist, but have a kind of anomalous, statistical subsistence; our moral and imaginative view of the world is no more affected by them than by the occupants of some home for the mentally deficient a little farther along the road. . . .

Oscar Wilde's wittily paradoxical statement about Nature's imitation of Art is literally true when the Nature is human nature and the Art that of television, radio, motion pictures, popular magazines. Life is so, people are so, the Medium shows its audience, and most of the audience believe it, expect people to be so, try to be so themselves. For them the People of the Medium are reality, what human beings normally, primarily are: and mere local or personal variations are not real in the same sense. The Medium mediates between us and raw reality, and the mediation more and more replaces reality for us. In many homes either the television set or the radio is turned on most of the time the family is awake. (Many radio stations have a news broadcast every half hour, and many people like and need to hear it.) It is as if the people longed to be established in reality, to be reminded continually of the "real," the "objective" world—the created world of the Medium—rather than be left at the mercy of actuality, of the helpless contingency of the world in which the radio receiver or television set is sitting. . . .

The world of events and celebrities and performers, the Great World, has become for many listeners, lookers, readers, the world of primary reality: how many times they have sighed at the colorless unreality of their own lives and families, sighed for the bright reality of, say, Lucille Ball's—of some shadow dyed, gowned, directed, produced, and agented into a being as equivocal as that of the square root of minus one. The watchers call the celebrities by their first names, approve or disapprove of "who they're dating," handle them with a mixture of love, identification, envy, and contempt—for the Medium has given its people so terrible a familiarity with everyone that it takes great magnanimity of spirit not to be affected by it. These celebrities are not heroes to us, their valets.

Better to have these real ones play themselves, and not sacrifice too much of their reality to art; better to have the watcher play himself, and not lose too much of himself in art. Usually the watcher is halfway between two worlds, paying full attention to neither: half distracted from, half distracted by, this distraction— and able for the moment not to be affected too greatly, have too great demands made upon him, by either world. For in the Medium, which we escape to from work, nothing is ever *work,* nothing ever makes intellectual or emotional or imaginative demands which we might find it difficult to satisfy. . . .

Our age is an age of nonfiction; of gossip columns, interviews, photographic essays, documentaries; of articles, condensed or book length, spoken or written; of real facts about real people. Art lies to us to tell the (sometimes disquieting) truth; the Medium tells us truths, facts, in order to make us believe some reassuring or entertaining lie or half truth. These actually existing celebrities, of universally admitted importance, about whom we are told directly authoritative facts—how can fictional characters compete with them? These *are* our fictional characters, our Lears and Clytemnestras. (This is ironically appropriate, since many of their doings and sayings are fictional, made up by public relations officers, columnists, agents, or other affable familiar ghosts.) And the Medium gives us such facts, such photographs, such tape recordings, such clinical reports not only about the great, but also about (representatives samples of) the small; when we have been shown so much about so many—*can* be shown, we feel, anything about anybody—does fiction seem so essential as it once seemed? Shakespeare or Tolstoy can show us all about someone, but so can *Life;* and when *Life* does, it's someone real.

The Medium is half life and half art, and competes with both life and art. It spoils its audience for both; spoils both for its audience. For the People of the Medium life isn't sufficiently a matter of success and glamour and celebrity, isn't entertaining enough, distracting enough, *mediated* enough; and art is too difficult or individual or novel, too restrained or indirect, too much a matter of tradition and the past, of special attitudes and aptitudes: its mediation sometimes is queer or excessive, and sometimes is not even recognizable as mediation. The Medium's mixture of rhetoric and reality, which gives people what we know they want in the form we know they like, is something more efficient and irresistible, more habit-forming, than any art. . . .

The Medium represents to the artist all that he has learned not to do: its sure-fire stereotypes seem to him what any true art, true spirit, has had to struggle past on its way to the truth. The artist sees the values and textures of this art substitute replacing those of his art with most of society, conditioning the expectations of what audience he has kept. . . . It is no wonder that the professional who writes the ordinary commercial success, the ordinary script, scenario, or article, resembles imaginative writers less than he resembles advertising agents, columnists, editors, and producers. He is a technician who can supply a standard product, a rhetorician who can furnish a regular stimulus for a regular response, what has always made the dog salivate in this situation. He is the opposite of the imaginative artist: instead of stubbornly or helplessly sticking to what he sees and feels, to what seems right for him, true to reality, regardless of what the others think and want, he gives the others what they think and want, regardless of what he himself sees and feels.

Mass culture either corrupts or isolates the writer. His old feeling of oneness, of speaking naturally to an audience with essentially similar standards, is gone; and writers do not any longer have much of the consolatory feeling that took its place, the feeling of writing for the happy few, the kindred spirits whose standards are those of the future. (Today they feel: the future, should there be one, will be worse.) True works of art are more and more produced away from, in opposition to, society. And yet the artist needs society as much as society needs him: as our cultural enclaves get smaller and drier, more hysterical or academic, one mourns for the artists inside them and the public outside. . . .

Even if the rebellious artist's rebellion is whole-hearted, it can never be whole-stomached, whole-Unconscious'd. Part of him wants to be like his kind, is like his kind; longs to be loved and admired and successful. Our society (and the artist, in so far as he is truly a part of it) has no place set aside for the different and poor and obscure, the fools for Christ's sake: they all go willy-nilly into Limbo. The artist is tempted, consciously, to give his society what it wants, or if he won't or can't, to give it nothing at all; is tempted, unconsciously, to give it superficially independent or contradictory works which are at heart works of the Medium. (Tennessee Williams' *Sweet Bird of Youth* is far less like Chekhov than it is like Mickey Spillane.) It is hard to go on serving both God and Mammon when God is so really ill-, Mammon so really well-organized. Shakespeare wrote for the Medium of his day; if Shakespeare were alive now he'd be writing *My Fair Lady;* isn't *My Fair Lady,* then, our *Hamlet?* shouldn't you be writing *Hamlet* instead of sitting there worrying about your superego? I need my *Hamlet!* So society speaks to the artist; but after he has written it its *Hamlet,* it tries to make sure that he will never do it again. There are more urgent needs that it wants him to satisfy: to lecture to it; to make public appearances; to be interviewed; to be on television shows; to give testimonials; to make trips abroad for the State Department; to judge books for contests or book clubs; to read for publishers, judge for publishers, be a publisher for publishers; to be an editor; to teach writing at colleges or writers' conferences; to write scenarios or scripts or articles, articles about his home town for *Holiday,* about cats or clothes or Christmas for *Vogue,* about "How I Wrote *Hamlet*" for anything; to . . .

But why go on? I once heard a composer, lecturing, say to a poet, lecturing: "They'll pay us to do *anything,* so long as it isn't writing music or writing poems." I knew the reply that, as a member of my society, I should have made: "So long as they pay you, what do you care?" But I didn't make it—it was plain that they cared. . . . But how many more learn not to care, love what they once endured! . . .

The climate of our culture is changing. Under these new rains, new suns, small things grow great, and what was great grows small; whole species disappear and are replaced. The American present is very different from the American past: so different that our awareness of the extent of the changes has been repressed, and we regard as ordinary what is extraordinary (ominous perhaps) both for us and the rest of the world. For the American present is many other peoples' future: our cultural and economic example is, to much of the world, mesmeric, and it is only its weakness and poverty that prevent it from hurrying with us into the Roman future. Yet at this moment of our greatest power and success, our thought and art are full of troubled gloom, of the conviction of our own decline. When the president of Yale University writes that "the ideal of the good life has faded from the educational process, leaving only miscellaneous prospects of jobs and joyless hedonism," are we likely to find it unfaded among our entertainers and executives? Is the influence of what I have called the Medium likely to make us lead any good life? to make us love and try to attain any real excellence, beauty, magnanimity? or to make us understand these as obligatory but transparent rationalizations, behind which the realities of money and power are waiting?

Matthew Arnold once spoke about our green culture in terms that have an altered relevance (but are not yet irrelevant) to our ripe one. He said: "What really dissatisfies in American civilization is the want of the *interesting,* a want due chiefly to the want of those two great elements of the interesting, which are elevation and beauty." This use of *interesting* (and, perhaps, this tone of a curator pointing out what is plain and culpable) shows how far along in the decline of the West Arnold came; it is only in the latter days that we ask to be interested. He had found the word in Carlyle. Carlyle is writing to a friend to persuade him not to emigrate to the United States; he asks, "Could you banish yourself from all that is interesting to your mind, forget the history, the glorious institutions, the noble principles of old Scotland—that you might eat a better dinner, perhaps?" We smile, and feel like reminding Carlyle of the history, the glorious institutions, the noble principles of new America, that New World which is, after all, the heir of the Old. And yet . . . Can we smile as comfortably, today, as we could have smiled yesterday? listen as unconcernedly, if on taking leave of us some tourist should say, with the penetration and obtuseness of his kind:

I remember reading somewhere: that which you inherit from your fathers you must earn in order to possess. I have been so much impressed with your power and possessions that I have neglected, perhaps, your principles. The elevation or beauty of your spirit did not equal, always, that of your mountains and skyscrapers: it seems to me that your society provides you with "all that is interesting to your mind" only exceptionally, at odd hours, in little reservations like those of your Indians. But as for your dinners, I've never seen anything like them: your daily bread come *flambé*. And yet—wouldn't you say?—the more dinners a man eats, the more comfort he possesses, the hungrier and more uncomfortable some part of him becomes: inside every fat man there is a man who is starving. Part of you is being starved to death, and the rest of you is being stuffed to death. . . . But this will change: no one goes on being stuffed to death or starved to death forever.

This is a gloomy, an equivocal conclusion? Oh yes, I come from an older culture, where things are accustomed to coming to such conclusions; where there is no last-paragraph fairy to bring one, always, a happy ending—or that happiest of all endings, no ending at all. And have I no advice to give you, as I go? None. You are too successful to need advice, or to be able to take it if it were offered; but if ever you should fail, it is there waiting for you, the advice or consolation of all the other failures.

IV. RECREATIONAL LEADERSHIP AND PRIVATE AGENCIES

EDITOR'S INTRODUCTION

Opportunities are plentiful in the new and expanding profession of recreation. Formal education and training date only from 1926. Moreover, it was not until 1960 that a significant number of universities provided undergraduate and graduate instruction leading to special degrees in recreation. In that year there were more than 2,500 students in this field and 648 degrees were granted.

Students seeking a field of endeavor that will satisfy one of America's needs may want to consider the formal study of recreation. The educational requirements for professional work in recreation and its objectives and personnel standards are described in the first of the two articles in this section. The second article surveys the various types of private organizations which are engaged in recreational work. Federal and state activities are reviewed in Section II, and an example of recreationists working in a municipal program appears in "Municipal Sports Fitness Camps" in Section III. below.

RECREATION AS A PROFESSION [1]

The profession [of recreation] is actively trying to prescribe its boundaries and horizons. For many years, the profession has tried to make recreation explicit and distinct, separate from education, medicine, social welfare, and other related areas. The hazard to avoid, of course, is making it so general that it has no meaning, or so specific that we fragment and splinter and lose effectiveness. The result of either would be lack of public under-

[1] From *The Leisure Age: Its Challenge to Recreation*, by Norman P. Miller and Duane M. Robinson. © 1963. By Wadsworth Publishing Company, Inc., Belmont, California. Reprinted by permission of the publisher. p 381-404. Norman P. Miller is associate professor of physical education, University of California, Los Angeles, and Duane M. Robinson is professor of sociology, George Williams College.

standing and support for aims and objectives. Lay participation on boards and commissions and in the organization of community coordinating and recreation councils is doing much to build public understanding, but this must be broadened considerably if the profession is to have full support of the general public for its philosophy and goals. . . .

Code of Ethics

The American Recreation Society, the Group-Work Section of the National Association of Social Workers, the National Recreation Association, and the American Institute of Park Executives have adopted codes of ethics; numerous state recreation societies have followed suit. These codes are fairly similar in nature and spell out the recreation worker's responsibilities to (1) *participants*, through belief in and treatment of them fairly as individuals, (2) *society*, through promotion of democratic processes, loyalty, and improvement of community life, (3) *the profession*, through giving of best efforts to it, participating actively in professional organizations, and contributing to its advancement, (4) *self*, through objectivity, maintenance of fitness, and respect for others, and (5) *agency*, through loyalty, adherence to rules and regulations, cooperation, and maintenance of a professional level of service.

[Paul] Douglass, in his "Guide for Leisure Leaders on the Space Frontier" [*California Recreation News and Previews*, February 1958] suggests these goals:

Grow intellectually to a fuller understanding of the [leisure-space] age by carefully selected reading and thoughtful discussion.

Mature spiritually by rethinking the goals of living in the context of the leisure-space age.

Elevate programs from routine insignificance and let them speak the idiom of the age.

Develop teamwork in mind-outreaching, soul-satisfying projects which combine the resources of libraries, museums, craft centers, discussion groups, and value-defining activity.

Have courage to budget your time and resources to the significant.

Elevate the standards of the profession by active participation in professional societies.

Strengthen the channels of public information so that people will understand your goals, the resources which you make available, and the satisfactions which they may enjoy.

Realize that the learning process may function at its best in leisure pursuits, the recreation leader being thus the most responsible of all teachers.

Look to the future with personal expectation and work to make the "ought to be" the "is."

Be imaginative in encouraging growth in the habits of participant citizenship.

Specialized Body of Knowledge

Fundamental to professional status is the accumulation and development of a specialized body of knowledge, complex enough to require special education and with sufficient intellectual content that scholarship is necessary to master it. This criterion separates a craft from a profession. As [Roy] Sorenson says:

There will always be a large place in recreation for the craftsmen. We will use a large number of nonprofessional people as coaches, assistants on playgrounds, instructors, and in other ways. But those on the leadership level who need to know why as well as how, require a more complex body of knowledge. ["Professional Maturity," *American Recreation Society Quarterly Bulletin,* May 1953]

The foundations for the body of knowledge are found primarily in the natural and social sciences and the humanities. They include biology, psychology, anthropology, philosophy, and sociology. . . .

The specialized body of knowledge in recreation arises from the application of the foundation facts and understandings to the leisure setting. This body of knowledge comprises: the history, philosophy, and theories of leisure and recreation; facts and understandings of the role of leisure and recreation in the development of the individual; the social significance of leisure and recreation as a conditioner of culture; people's patterns of recreation and leisure; understandings in the areas of planning, organization, administration, and leadership related to programs of recreation; and facts concerning the dynamics of groups in meeting basic needs of individuals.

One of the challenges for the recreation profession is to extend the volume and depth of its specialized body of knowledge, but the necessary scholarship has been all too scarce within the ranks of the profession, primarily because professional education is still a new idea, and also because most practitioners have been satisfied with mere "know-how" rather than "know-why." Outside of the field, most research has been done by sociologists, psychologists, and therapists, as the literature reflects. . . .

The major focus of research efforts in past years can be grouped generally into six categories: (1) physical and mental health (experimentation with the use of recreation as a therapeutic tool and the adaptation of activities for therapeutic purposes), (2) evaluation of leadership-preparation programs, (3) outdoor recreation and the use of land and water areas for recreation purposes, (4) design of recreation facilities, equipment, and areas, (5) measurement of the effect of participation upon the individual (primarily within the industrial setting, and related to improving worker effectiveness on the job), and (6) development of measurement tools and devices for determining the effectiveness of recreation services. . . .

Methodology

The recreation environment usually is informal and playful, the attitude of the participant is one of freedom, and opportunity for choice exists. In almost no other social institution does this kind of environment prevail; the setting tends to be one of compulsion rather than of freedom. But in the recreation setting, the worker normally deals with people who want to be there and who have purpose. The worker's task is to help the individual achieve the special goals of leisure time, particularly seeking to guarantee creativity.

Out of this environment emerges the core method of working with individuals and groups in recreation. In certain areas of professional responsibility this methodology may vary in degree. For the face-to-face worker "on the firing line" it is the major component of his leadership tools. For the supervisor, specialist, or administrator it is an integral component, but it is supplemented by other methodology not necessarily unique to recreation. The specialist may use primarily a teaching methodology. The executive would use an administrative methodology primarily. All of these individuals work with people, however, and they have a common base or generic method. . . .

Professional Education

True professional education for recreation is a relatively new development. Prior to 1926, schools and colleges gave it only meager attention, but with the establishment of the National Recreation School by the National Recreation Association in that year the first real recreation curriculum came into being. During the 1930's, professional courses were introduced in a few colleges and universities, and following the first college conference (1937) on training recreation leaders, real emphasis was directed to the professional preparation of recreation personnel. The growth and expansion since then has been steady. In 1937 there were only five institutions offering recreation programs; by 1944 there were nineteen; and by 1960, there were sixty-two, with thirty-nine institutions offering graduate instruction and fifteen conferring the doctoral degree. In some states, junior colleges now offer professional and general education courses in recreation.

The number of students engaged in programs of professional education increases steadily. In 1960, [H. D.] Sessoms reported, 2,673 students were preparing for recreation careers and 684 degrees were granted. . . .

Varying patterns of organization have characterized the development of recreation education. . . . One approach, widely employed, was the development of curricula and courses around specific skills and abilities required for employment and on-the-job performance. The advantage of this approach was that curricula could be geared directly to demands in the field and for specific agencies or levels of leadership. In view of the rapidly broadening scope of leadership opportunities, however, it was an impractical approach because, as the recreation profession grew and matured, concepts and descriptions of the worker's task changed. The current approach is functional, one wherein the problems met by the worker in the performance of basic roles have been identified, the competencies needed to solve these problems have been delineated, and curricular experiences have been planned to develop these competencies.

There is increasing utilization of recreation courses by other disciplines. Examples of this are the addition of recreation education courses to physical education credential requirements, and the provision for recreation background in preparation programs in home economics, nursing, elementary education, and social welfare.

Undergraduate Preparation

It is generally accepted that undergraduate professional preparation for recreation should have three emphases: (1) A broad, liberal, cultural emphasis, encompassing foundation study in the humanities, social sciences, communicative arts, and the natural sciences, which would be designed to provide the student with a better understanding of himself and his relation to others in a constantly changing society. This is the general education content for the professional recreation worker and consensus is that it should constitute about half the curriculum. (2) A general professional emphasis directed to development of basic understandings and competencies in the fundamental areas of educational psychology, sociology, human growth and development, public administration, evaluation and research, group processes, and principles of administration and supervision. (3) A specialized professional emphasis geared to developing the specific competencies required in the worker role. In this area are the foundation experiences in the history, philosophy, and principles of leisure and recreation, program areas and methods of leadership, and organization and administration of services, supplemented with directed out-of-class field experiences designed to provide the preprofessional student with working knowledge of the tools and methodology of the professional worker. Specialization at the undergraduate level should be minimized and should focus primarily upon the development of the skills, understandings, and knowledges common to all recreation workers.

Graduate Preparation

Increasing attention and emphasis is being given to graduate preparation in the field of recreation, owing to the need for advanced study and research and the demand for preparation of leadership for higher-level positions in supervision, teaching, research, and administration. Graduate preparation presupposes that the student already possesses competence in the actual working relationship, developed through sound undergraduate preparation, field work, and experience on the job. Graduate study should build upon this background and national conferences have recommended three emphases: (1) further emphasis in the foundation areas of the history and philosophy of American culture, the impact of modern leisure on the lives of people and the understanding of the institutionalized forms that leisure and recreation are assuming; (2) emphasis upon increasing skill and understanding in the use of fundamental tools of evaluation and research and their applications to problem solving; and (3) opportunity for specialization in such areas as hospital, industry, and camping, and the development of competencies necessary for administrative and supervisorial positions. Field work at the graduate level is invaluable and internship programs have been developed to provide this.

The amount of graduate education necessary and the level of the degrees offered vary. Few public or private recreation agency positions throughout the country require advanced degrees although the job to be done may deserve it and demand it. If recreation is to gain full professional status, however, the professional education program must continue to raise its status within higher education, particularly at the doctoral level. This is critical for the development of an adequate research program and the enrichment and upgrading of college teaching faculties. . . .

Personnel Standards

The formulation and refining of personnel standards have received major attention from recreation professional organizations, agencies, and individuals for many years. The establishment of sound employment practices with adequate salaries, working conditions, job descriptions, educational requirements, recruitment, and identification procedures is part of the standards-implementation process.

Leadership Functions

The assumption is that recreation standards are based upon the functions the leader performs in achieving his major objective: assisting individuals to attain leisure values through recreative uses of their leisure time. What are these functions? [George D.] Butler identifies the following as typical:

1. Guide and encourage individuals to acquire new interests and to gain greater satisfaction from participation in familiar activities. 2. Help to organize recreation groups and to assure successful group operation. 3. Attempt to expand and equalize recreation opportunities. 4. Teach people to acquire new or more advanced skills. 5. Provide and maintain places in which individuals in groups may engage in activities. 6. Assure safe and healthful conditions and practices. 7. Furnish equipment and supplies essential for the enjoyment of many types of recreation. . . .

The exact number of professionally employed recreation workers in America is rather difficult to ascertain. Estimates have ranged from twenty to twenty-five thousand. These statistics were based upon projection of regional recreation studies that included leadership. Another picture has been provided through a national social-welfare manpower study made in 1960, which reported 116,000 social-welfare workers employed in the United States. Of these, 10,450 were recreation workers in government and voluntary agencies. Of these workers, 64 per cent were found in government agencies—52 per cent in state and local agencies and 12 per cent in Federal agencies. The remaining 36 per cent of the workers were employed in voluntary agencies. These figures were derived through sampling and probably do not include the commercial fields or fully reflect either the public or private agency. . . .

Leadership Qualifications

The general education experience and personal qualifications required for initial placement are basically the same, whether the agency is public or private, large or small. The differences and variations occur in salaries and in scope of responsibility.

The personal qualifications require that the potential recreation leader be enthusiastic, dependable, and of sound character; that he have a sense of humor, enjoy good health, be flexible, creative, and personally attractive; that he have broad interests, be friendly, like people, and be energetic and cooperative. . . . However, they are so general and have become so accepted as criteria for selection processes that it is more upon other bases that standards in the recreation profession are being largely determined. They are, in effect, the base point from which the other standards operate.

The most important standards are the educational requirements set for entrance into professional service in the field. The minimum essential is graduation from a recognized institution of higher education with a bachelor's degree, a major in recreation or in a closely allied field such as physical education, group work, education, or sociology, and including supervised field work in the recreation setting. Graduate study is necessary for persons preparing for or seeking advanced positions that also require experience. There are opportunities for specialists with degrees in the program areas of art, music, drama, and the like. Deviation from this standard has been dependent largely upon the supply of personnel available. Because of the relative newness of programs of professional recreation education, agencies are sometimes unable to secure leadership that meets these standards, but progress is being made. A survey of the education of these recreation workers showed that 53 per cent possessed bachelor's degrees or higher degrees. Fifty-one per cent of those in state and local governments had degrees, 38 per cent of those in Federal service had degrees, and 61 per cent of those in voluntary agencies had degrees.

Personnel Practices

Beginning salaries for recreation workers are comparable to the beginning salaries of allied professional groups—nursing, teaching, social work, and so on. The exact amount is usually dependent upon the size and type of agency and the part of the country in which it is located. By and large, public recreation agencies tend to pay higher salaries than private agencies, and salaries are higher in larger cities than in smaller cities, regardless of whether the agency is public or private. The salary scale in recreation reflects the local market. A study of salary levels showed that the median annual salary for all recreation workers was $4,500. The median salary for those with bachelor's degrees was $5,240. The median salary for those holding master's degrees was $6,900 annually. . . .

Professional Associations

The recreation profession has organized itself into many professional societies and associations. . . . Each of the major organizations has members who identify primarily with the area of concern of the organization.

The major groups are: (1) the American Association for Health, Physical Education, and Recreation, composed chiefly of physical educators and school recreation personnel; (2) the

American Camping Association, composed of individuals and agencies interested in private and organizational camps and camp programs; (3) the American Recreation Society, composed primarily of public recreation workers; (4) the American Institute of Park Executives, made up largely of park personnel; (5) the Association of College Unions with institutional memberships, including those individuals responsible for the operation of college union programs and facilities; (6) the Group Work Section of the National Association of Social Workers, consisting mainly of private agency workers; (7) the National Conference on State Parks, composed essentially of state park executives; (8) the National Industrial Recreation Association, with a membership made up largely of individuals and companies with employee recreation programs; and (9) the Society of State Directors of Health, Physical Education, and Recreation, with a membership of past and present staffs of state departments of health, physical education, and recreation.

In addition, there are two major service organizations; namely, the Athletic Institute and the National Recreation Association. The former is a nonprofit organization whose purpose is to promote and encourage participation in the field of athletics, recreation, physical education, and health education. It is supported by the manufacturers and distributors of athletic, sports, and recreation goods. The National Recreation Association has long been identified as one of the major leaders in the recreation movement, and performs many functions common to professional societies with membership open to both organizations and individuals, and has a full-time professional consultant staff that renders nationwide field services.

PRIVATE RECREATIONAL AGENCIES [2]

The community recreation program includes activities that are provided by semipublic and private organizations as well as

[2] From *Leisure and Recreation—A Study of Leisure and Recreation in Their Sociological Aspects,* Third Edition, by Martin H. Neumeyer and Esther S. Neumeyer. Copyright © 1958 The Ronald Press Company, New York. p 378-419. Reprinted by permission. Dr. Martin H. Neumeyer is professor emeritus of sociology, University of Southern California.

by public agencies. The earliest organizations for leisure in America were chiefly of a private or semipublic nature. These and commercial amusements often preceded public provision for recreation. Many communities, especially in rural areas, have no local public facilities for recreation even today. . . .

Recreational Agencies for Youth

Out of the welter of social welfare, religious, educational, and recreational trends that marked the end of the nineteenth century, boys' and girls' clubs of the modern type emerged. Since the beginning of the twentieth century such clubs have multiplied rapidly under various auspices. [M. M.] Chambers describes the membership, purposes, activities, and finances of some two hundred and fifty organizations as reported by their headquarters offices, embracing not only the youth-membership associations having a majority of their membership under the age of twenty-five, but also a great many adult organizations concerned in part with youth.

Youth-serving agencies and group work have undergone many changes during recent years. . . . The center of interest has shifted from program building to personality development and adjustment. The program of activities is planned to meet specific needs of the individual participants in accordance with their capacities. This is sometimes called the individual approach to group work. Group work and case work are closely related. When a program of activities is designed to help the individuals attain the ends of social adjustment and personality growth, then case procedure is needed to ascertain needs and to deal with individual problems. At the same time, group work is thought of as a process whereby individuals become socialized and are made an integral part of a dynamic on-going life.

Y Organizations

The Y organizations are the oldest of the outstanding associations sponsoring group work today; but the Boys' Work of the YMCA and the Y-Teens (formerly Girl Reserves) of the YWCA are of relatively recent origin. The work of these organizations has expanded during recent years and has undergone constant changes. Their primary purpose is to advance the physical, intellectual, social, moral, and spiritual interests of young men and women and to associate them with Christian living. . . . The leisure-time activities include socials, entertainments, dances, dramatics, musical events, and movies; health and physical education, gymnasium activities, sports, games, and field events; informal education through clubs, forums, discussion groups, and reading material; and the more formal classes on various subjects. Constructive leisure-time activities are stressed, including those that provide opportunities for sociability, friendships, and character development, as well as the purely recreational pursuits.

The work for boys has grown steadily in relative importance. A wide range of organized groups have been fostered—Bible study classes, hobby and interest groups, teams, school clubs (notably Hi-Y, Junior Hi-Y, and Gray-Y), church clubs, clubs for working boys, neighborhood clubs, and many others. Originally, these activities were organized around the interests that centered in the YMCA buildings, but now they are built around interests wherever found. Instead of encouraging boys to travel great distances to the Y buildings, the leaders go into the community and organize clubs in schools, churches, playgrounds, or wherever suitable facilities can be found. Seldom is a preconceived program used; an effort is made to build the program around the natural interests of the boys. Summer camps, boys' conferences, father-and-son banquets, athletics and sports, hobby events, and counseling services are some of the distinctive aspects of the work with boys. . . . The association movement has always been closely identified with churches. . . .

The program of the YWCA has closely paralleled that of the YMCA Associations. The Y-Teen program has become one of the most important functions of the YWCA. Y-Teens are the organization's young or junior members, usually girls of high-school age. The program is not rigidly fixed; it is an idea and a general program that can and should be adapted to the needs of the particular group of girls. The leaders have avoided preconceived programing and have shunned awards and individual honors as means of stimulating interest. This does not mean that there is no program and that there are no insignia. Materials and aids are provided, but the aim is to utilize the natural interests of the girls, to discover and meet their needs, and to build up a program that will enable the girls to face life squarely and to find and give the best.

The YMHA and YWHA are the Jewish organizations which are comparable to the YMCA and YWCA. These organizations offer recreation in the local communities. Jewish groups have established community centers, camps, . . . and other agencies to meet the recreation needs of their constituents.

Boy and Girl Scout Organizations

The scouting program is an idea and a movement rather than merely an organization. It originated in England as a definite movement about 1907 and 1908. . . . The American organization of the Boy Scouts was founded in 1910, and the Girl Scouts in 1912. Scout troops were designed to supplement existing organizations—the home, the school, and the church—by engaging boys and girls in outdoor games and activities of cultural and practical value. A large proportion of the troops are organized in connection with other agencies.

The purpose of the Boy Scouts is to develop character and to train for citizenship by developing the boys' ability to do things for themselves and for others, by training them in scoutcraft, by teaching them patriotism, courage, self-reliance and kindred traits, and by developing strong bodies and physical fitness. Emphasis is placed on the "Scout Oath," which every boy must take before becoming a scout. He promises on his honor to do his duty to God and his country and to keep the Scout Law, to help others at all times, and to keep himself physically strong, mentally awake, and morally straight. The scout motto is "Be Prepared." Boy Scouts are expected to be trustworthy, loyal, helpful, friendly, courteous, kind, obedient, cheerful, thrifty, brave, clean, and reverent.

Among the activities usually provided by local councils are vocational exploration in over one hundred subjects; scoutcraft, especially woodcraft, handicraft, campcraft, signaling, nature lore, and trail building; health and safety, notably personal hygiene, lifesaving, first aid, and prevention of accidents; games and sports; and civic service, patriotism, and citizenship training. The boy passes from one rank to another by passing a series of tests, advancing from tenderfoot to second-class rank, and then to first-class rank. Merit badges are won along the way.

The organization of the Boy Scouts is quite simple. Boys must be twelve years old to be eligible for membership in the organization proper. The Cub Scout program is for boys from nine to eleven years old, and the Sea Scouts include boys fifteen years old and over. The Scouters are leaders eighteen years of age and over. A patrol consists of about eight boys, and a troop is made up of patrols, the number depending upon the natural grouping of the boys. The scoutmaster is the leader of the scout troop.

The scout program has been criticized for being too nationalistic and militaristic, too costly, and lacking in flexibility in its programs. The supporters of the movement contend that the system is unique, challenging, and fundamentally sound in organization. The boys meet in their own localities and usually are organized in cooperation with existing community institutions. The program is so comprehensive that it takes in all the major interests of boys of scout age.

The Girl Scout program is similar to that of the Boy Scouts. Girl Scouts are found over the entire world, following substantially the same program, but making adjustments to national traditions and cultural characteristics. All take the same oath, are governed by the same fundamental laws, and use the same motto, signs, and salutes. The patrol system is used, and progress is made through stages of tenderfoot, second-class, and first-class ranks. In the United States, the Girl Scout program is composed of activities and skills through which the girl reaches out toward many important aspects of life. With such a wide program, special talents have a chance to find expression and the girls find something of interest which will stimulate them in achieving honors and preparing themselves for life. . . . The total membership is extensive, including the three groups: Brownie Scouts (girls aged seven to nine), Intermediate Scouts (girls aged ten to fourteen), and Senior Scouts (girls aged fifteen to eighteen). Adult members of the organization serve as troop leaders, and committee and council members.

Other Youth Service Agencies

It is not possible to discuss in detail all of the other important youth-serving agencies or youth organizations, but a few of the more commonly known organizations will be described briefly.

A number of these organizations are chiefly interested in various crafts, Indian lore, and outdoor activities. Ernest Thompson Seton was the chief early pioneer of woodcraft. The Woodcraft League of America, which was established in 1902, was outstanding in the promotion of nature and Indian lore, campcraft, handicraft, homecraft, and various forms of sports and games. Woodcraft organizations, or Woodcraft Rangers as they are called in some localities, have no military features, their fees are nominal, they use the recreational approach rather than competition to stimulate interest, and they provide honors as awards for achievements in the progressive steps of the program. The tribes of both the Big Lodge and the Little Lodge are small, with an adult leader for each.

Camp Fire Girls, the organization founded by Dr. and Mrs. Luther H. Gulick in 1910, recognizes the importance of the intelligent use of leisure and has planned programs of activities designed to attract the interest of adolescent girls, encouraging them to embark upon a voyage of discovery through seven crafts —homecraft, health craft, handicraft, nature lore, camping, business, and citizenship. Girls are given duties and training in these fields of endeavor. Each unit is supervised by an adult leader—"Guarding of the Camp Fire." These leaders, directed by regional and national executives, supervise the girls through three stages of achievement: woodgathering, firemaking, and torchbearing. The spirit of service is fostered along feminine lines, and the activities are planned to train girls for duties that they must later assume in modern society.

The designation Boys' Club has been applied to those organizations in American cities that are associated with the Boys' Club of America, Inc., to distinguish a definite type of social service institution enrolling boy members under adult leadership. A club of boys was established in Hartford as early as 1861, and the name Boys' Club was applied to an organization of boys in New York in 1876. A number of Boys' Clubs have continued operation for more than fifty years. These organizations have specialized in work with boys. While they differ in their policies and programs, certain similarities have grown out of the sameness of boys' needs and interests, rather than through arbitrary standardization.

The chief features of Boys' Clubs are: regular membership; paid personnel, a staff of workers who have specialized in various types of boys' work; self-government and discipline; a club building, with games room, gym, and other facilities for physical activities; health services, vocational classes, club groups, a library and reading room, and facilities for music and drama, entertainments and celebrations. Many having camping facilities and emphasize outdoor activities. Counseling and guidance, citizenship, and character training are emphasized. The Boys' Club of America, Inc., supplies national leadership, publications and materials, and renders special services to local Boys' Clubs. It was originally organized in 1906 as the Federated Boys' Clubs.

Some Boys' Clubs have been set up especially for certain classes of boys, as is true of Boston's now famous Burroughs Newsboys Foundation and its affiliated Agassiz Village in the wilds of Maine. . . . Similar organizations, either local or more general, have been established to promote work with both boys and girls.

Various kinds of youth centers, often called Teen Centers or Teen-Age Centers, have sprung up during recent years in various places and under different kinds of auspices. Some of the early clubs were self-motivated groups, organized by and for youth, allowing greater participation by the young people in the management and control of the center. Some have lacked planned programs, with members doing pretty much what they pleased. Dancing was the main activity. Youth centers are places (rooms or buildings) equipped for the use of teen-agers. While originally some of the teen-age centers or canteens sprang up independently, without much adult supervision, the general tendency has been for these centers to become integrated with the programs of community recreation agencies. Their success has impressed community leaders that there is a need for more and better opportunities for youth, that young people have the capacity and the willingness to assume greater responsibility for the planning and carrying on of the program, and that there are values in letting youth organizations manage their own affairs.

The American Junior Red Cross, which is the junior membership of the American National Red Cross, was started in 1917. While its objectives are chiefly good health, intelligent citizenship, education, international understanding, and service, it has promoted certain forms of recreation.

Various agricultural and rural life organizations promote recreation among rural people. Of the youth agencies, many of which are sponsored by the Agricultural Extension Service of the Federal, state, and county governments, the most outstanding organizations are the 4-H Clubs and the Future Farmers of America. The membership and participation in these organizations are extensive. Individual and group projects are conducted, and recreation is an essential part of their programs. The American Farm Bureau and the National Grange have also sponsored organizations and projects for young people.

In addition to the organizations described, many other agencies serve youth or are organizations for youth. Youth-serving agencies have been coordinated on the national, regional, and local bases. The United Service Organizations (USO), councils of social agencies (or metropolitan planning councils), coordinating councils, and various youth committees or councils are examples of cooperative efforts in behalf of youth. The total membership in youth-serving agencies is not exactly known, but the major ones reach millions of young people and children. . . .

Recreational Organizations for Adults

While the major efforts of public and semipublic agencies to provide community recreation are in the interests of children and young people, adults are not entirely neglected. . . .

Industrial and Business Groups

Industrial recreation has been in existence in the United States for several decades. Even before World War I it was considered an important part of industrial welfare work and a potent factor in creating [a] better employer-employee relationship. Under the impetus of World War I, competitive athletics and the development of facilities for recreation in plants were encouraged. The 1920's witnessed a steady growth of recreation sponsored by employees, employers, or both. During the Depression, many of the programs were eliminated or curtailed. With the growth of unionization during the latter part of the 1930's, and with a changed attitude of management and unions toward the place of recreation in industry, recreation was given a new impetus. During World War II, with the rapid expansion of plants and personnel, the need to build and maintain workers' morale became urgent. As a result, industrial recreation gained rapidly, with increased cooperation of management and employees, a wider range of activities, and programs directed by trained leaders. The activities are increasingly being organized on the basis of interests, and the employees have a much larger share in the management of the program, with part of the cost borne by them.

Industrial recreation refers to pleasurable and noncompulsory activities engaged in for their own sake, carried on for the employees in industry and business during their free time, and sponsored by employers or jointly by employers and employees. While the main purpose is to provide wholesome leisure-time activities for the workers, giving them a chance to relax and to participate in enjoyable activities, industrial recreation has been recognized as an important factor in strengthening the physical and mental health of the workers, in creating good *esprit de corps* and morale in plants, in improving efficiency of production, in bringing about better employer-employee relations and cooperation, in lessening absenteeism and labor turnover, and in providing opportunities for creative expression and the development of leadership abilities. . . .

In some plants the program of recreation is administered entirely by the employees; in others it is sponsored and directed by the employers; and in others it is a cooperative enterprise in which both employers and employees share in the management and expenses. In some plants the recreation program is independent of other departments or divisions, whereas in others it is an adjunct of the personnel or industrial relations division, or is handled by labor-management committees. The number of employees and the size of the plant have a great deal to do with the kind of recreation program that can be put into operation. Large plants can afford to have broader programs and employ paid leaders, provided the management and the workers are favorably inclined. Smaller plants must depend upon volunteer leaders or part-time paid leaders. . . .

The recreation programs are financed in a number of ways, chiefly by direct contributions from the company or through a company benefit association, employee contributions, paid admissions and entry fees, concessions, union dues, and various . . . [other] devices for raising money. . . .

The major activities conducted by plants and by employee groups outside include athletics; . . . social and club activities, notably dancing, musical groups, dramatics, movies, hobby groups, bridge and [other] card games, chess and checkers, fashion shows, dinners and banquets; and . . . special outings, picnics, hunting trips, fishing, camping, and gardening (stressed during World War II). . . .

The chief causes of inadequate programs of recreation are the lack of company equipment and facilities, the lack of a diversified program to meet the varied needs of employees, insufficient numbers of employees or the employees living too far away from the plant, inadequate financing of the program, and lack of good leadership. The attitude of both employers and employees, including labor unions, is very important. If one or the other of these groups assumes a hostile attitude toward recreation, it is difficult to inaugurate and maintain the program. But in spite of the difficulties, industrial recreation is here to stay, and it will undoubtedly grow in extent and importance.

Many other types of occupational groups besides industrial and business organizations carry on forms of recreation. Labor unions have recreation programs of their own. . . . Various professional groups, government employees, especially in city police and fire departments, and mutual benefit organizations of various occupational groups have some recreation, not only for themselves but for their families as well. . . .

Athletic, Service, and Other Organizations

A great variety of clubs and voluntary associations have been organized for the purpose of recreation and social service. A wide range of functions and many different kinds of activities with a recreational or cultural emphasis are carried on.

Athletic clubs usually are exclusive, except that the facilities may be used on occasion by outside groups. Many of these clubs have expensive buildings with facilities for dining, dancing, physical recreation, sports and active games, quiet indoor games, reading, club meetings, and beauty culture; many have hotel accommodations and some have golf courses and beach equipment. Membership is usually expensive and largely for the wealthy. Specialized clubs, notably tennis and golf clubs, are organized for those interested in specific sports. However, not all members are interested in active athletics. These places frequently serve for lounging and resting purposes. Golf courses are commonly operated for members, but some are open to nonmembers upon payment of the established fee. . . .

Lodges and other secret societies have social and recreational functions, and some have luxurious headquarters with equipment for dining and social and recreational activities. The prominence given to ceremony and ritual gives them a distinct character. Secret societies perform religious services, and sometimes political and social reform functions. . . .

Service clubs, notably the Rotary, Kiwanis, Lions, and Optimist, are nonpolitical and nonsectarian civic organizations composed of representative business and professional men, whose purpose is both recreation and service. An attempt is made to recognize community needs, to discover ways of meeting them, and, either by direct effort or in cooperation with other organizations, to help solve problems. Interest in special projects is often stimulated by such clubs. Many clubs are interested in boys' and girls' work in the community and give financial and other support to group work agencies. . . .

The monthly noonday luncheon is usually the chief function. Programs are usually snappy, consisting of a lecture on some topic of vital interest, music, business, announcements of events, interspersed with jokes and teasing, and assessing fines for various reasons. The fines are means of raising money for projects. The joviality and constant laughter make these meetings happy occasions for good times, as well as for business and programs. The American Legion and similar veterans' organizations may be classed, from the point of view of recreation, with service organizations. Their functions are political, patriotic, service, and recreational.

Women's clubs have broad programs, including some recreation, but with a strong emphasis on cultural and community service undertakings. Their original aim was to attain culture and refinement, and the programs were predominantly literary and artistic. The trend is away from the preoccupation solely with literature, art, and music, toward placing a greater emphasis on community and civic affairs. The social side of women's clubs, though important, has not usurped the leading role. The progressive clubs give members "something to think about" and expect them to render various kinds of services. Lectures, classes, reading circles, dramatics, and art exhibits are provided, and the larger ones have libraries, community theaters, gymnasiums, and many other types of facilities. . . .

Drama groups are fairly numerous, composed chiefly of amateurs and voluntary helpers. Various kinds of theaters, commonly known as community, art, or little theaters, have been organized to promote amateur dramatics. . . .

Religious Recreational Groups

Modern progressive church leaders feel that, while religious worship and education are the chief functions of the church, recreational and social activities and social services are important and integral parts of the church program. The worship services, religious education, recreation, and service activities should be integrated, for all are a part of the total program of the church. . . .

What forms of recreation activities are usually carried on by local churches? That depends upon the equipment of the churches, their location, the needs of their members and constituents, their emphasis, and the quality of leadership which they possess. Some churches have community houses fully equipped for a variety of recreation pursuits, while others may have the barest of facilities. The socially oriented churches try to meet the recreation needs of the people in one way or another.

Games, parties, socials, entertainments, teas, dinners, dramatics, musical events, club work, and in some churches dancing and sports are the chief church-centered activities. Boys' and girls' clubs, young people's organizations, and to some extent the women's and men's organizations are the groups in which much of the recreation takes place. A church with a gymnasium has a chance to conduct various kinds of games and sports, athletic events, and similar activities. . . .

An auditorium with a stage is now considered a necessity in a modern church. Dramatics, pageants, musicals, and festivals are more and more being conducted by church groups. The educational and religious values of dramatic art and music can hardly be overestimated, provided they are properly directed. Religious leaders increasingly appreciate the tremendous potential force in dramatic presentation of religious and moral themes. Ceremonials and church liturgy have always been full of dramatic presentations. Choral and instrumental music, including congregational singing, is an integral part of church services.

Some churches have motion picture equipment. Audiovisual education is now considered an important phase of general education, and churches are increasingly making use of still and motion pictures as a part of religious education and the recreational program. . . .

Although the equipment may be meager, with competent leadership much good can be accomplished through club groups. Equipment is less important than trained leadership. Church camps have been in existence for some time. Vacation schools involve a considerable amount of recreation. Thus, throughout the year, especially during the summer vacation, churches are providing recreation for the boys and girls as well as the youth of the community.

It is difficult to apply religious ideals to the recreation program. Recreation is an activity carried on during leisure for enjoyment. To have fun is about all that most people are concerned about when they engage in recreational pursuits. However, leaders in this field often apply two additional ideals or ulterior tests: (1) Do the activities contribute to the enrichment of personality and the development of character? The development of wholesome attitudes and clean habits and the improvement of human relations through socialized personalities are especially important in this connection. (2) Does the program contribute to community welfare? In other words, does the program make for a better community?. . .

Church Social Centers

In addition to the recreation activities in local churches, various kinds of institutions and agencies have been sponsored and supported by church organizations. The first outstanding efforts on the part of churches to sponsor recreation were in connection with social settlements, neighborhood houses, and institutional churches located in slum and blighted areas of cities. Toynbee Hall in London, which was established on the east side of the city in 1885, was the first social settlement in the world. The movement soon spread to America and progressed under the auspices of churches.

Some social settlements not only are poorly equipped for recreation but have insufficient funds to employ competent leaders. Others that are adequately equipped and have trained leaders are doing splendid work for the underprivileged people. A well-equipped social center has a gymnasium and possibly a swimming pool, a playground, facilities for club work, a library and a reading room, an auditorium with a stage for dramatics, equipment for music, and space for indoor and outdoor games. Group work and recreation activities now constitute the major part of the social settlement programs.

Institutional churches carry on a variety of activities designed to meet the needs of the people living in the vicinity of the church. Churches that are thoroughly adjusted to community needs open their facilities to neighborhood groups, shelter a variety of organizations regardless of creed or race, and have clinics for the medical and dental needs of the people. They carry on welfare and recreation programs, as well as religious and educational schedules. Many of the missions and institutional churches in the slum areas of cities carry on a more extensive community program and more definitely adjust their program to meet the needs of the underprivileged people than do the larger churches in the better residential areas.

Social centers are broader in scope than institutions sponsored by churches, but church organizations have been active in supplying the funds, the personnel, and the general management of such centers in congested urban areas. Many of the community chest agencies are, directly or indirectly, under church auspices. Recreation is usually one of their functions.

Local churches, as well as the special community center, have been the focal points of a variety of activities. For a great number of people, the church has been the main source of social and recreational activities. Commercial amusements provided diversions away from the church and competed with it. The trend now is toward a greater endeavor on the part of churches to meet the needs of the people, including social affairs and recreational activities. The forms of church-centered recreation are changing. To be successful, any church-centered program of recreation must be geared to the needs and interests of the people. Modern churches have established organizations to meet the special needs of children and young people and have utilized the services of other organizations for youth.

Church Youth Organizations

From the point of view of total membership and services, church youth organizations are possibly the most outstanding organizations for youth. A brief survey of the Protestant, Catholic, and Jewish youth-serving agencies will illustrate the extent of these organizations and their major objectives.

Protestant organizations. The Protestant youth-serving organizations are by far the most numerous, partly because of the many denominations. The International Society of Christian Endeavor and the Methodist Youth Fellowship have the largest memberships. The former has approximately a million and a half members in eighty thousand local societies affiliated with eighty-seven Christian denominations in all parts of the world. The chief purpose is to promote Christian life and mutual acquaintance among members and to train them for church and community work. The Methodist Youth Fellowship is a denominational organization for young people aged twelve to twenty-three, with a membership of over a million, designed to build Christian character, to develop friendships, to train leaders, and to promote social welfare.

Nearly all [other] Protestant denominations have similar organizations, emphasizing Christian education and character development, recreation, social service, and a variety of special functions. The activities, including social, athletic, and recreational functions, as well as the more strictly religious and educational endeavors, vary according to the denominational emphasis. Some are organized on the age-level basis, with separate organizations for children, young people (high school and college), and adults.

Catholic organizations. The Catholic Students' Mission Crusade and Sodality of Our Lady have the largest memberships, but such organizations as the Knights of Columbus (Boy Life Bureau), International Federation of Catholic Alumnae, the National Catholic Welfare Council, and the National Catholic Youth Council, as well as the various diocesan and local welfare and youth councils and agencies, reach into every community where Catholic churches exist. The religious emphasis is predominant, but a wide range of recreational and social activities are carried on by most of them.

Jewish Organizations. B'nai B'rith Hillel Foundations, B'nai B'rith Youth Organization, Council of Jewish Federations and Welfare Funds, and the organizations associated with the national Jewish Welfare Board operate a variety of services to local Jewish groups, including social and recreational activities. The chief purpose of these and the other Jewish organizations is to serve the young people and adults of their own group, promoting recreational as well as religious, intellectual, and social welfare programs.

This is only a part of the program of youth organizations, for many churches make use of other youth-serving agencies, such as the Boy Scouts, Girl Scouts, Young Men's Christian Association, and Young Women's Christian Association.

BIBLIOGRAPHY

An asterisk (*) preceding a reference indicates that the article or a part of it has been reprinted in this book.

Books, Pamphlets, and Documents

Adams, J. T. Frontiers of American culture; a study of adult education. Scribner. New York. '44.

American Association for Health, Physical Education, and Recreation. Current administrative problems: athletics, health education, physical education and recreation; prepared under the chairmanship of Elmon L. Vernier. The association. 1201 16th St. Washington 6, D.C. '60.

American Federation of Labor-Congress of Industrial Organizations. Shorter work week. Public Affairs Press. Washington D.C. '57.

Anderson, Jackson. Industrial recreation: a guide to its organization and administration. McGraw. New York. '55.

*Anderson, Nels. Work and leisure. Free Press. New York. '62.

Arensberg, C. M. ed. Research in industrial human relations; a critical appraisal. Harper. New York. '57.

Bartlett, Sir Frederic. Mind at work and play. Beacon. Boston. '51.

Bell, Daniel. Work and its discontents. Beacon. Boston. '56.

Bernert, Eleanor. America's children. Wiley. New York. '58.

Blake, Peter. God's own junkyard; the planned deterioration of America's landscape. Holt. New York '64.

Brightbill, C. K. Man and leisure. Prentice-Hall. Englewood Cliffs, N.J. '61.

Brockman, C. F. Recreational use of wild lands. McGraw. New York. '59.

Brooks, Paul. Roadless area. Knopf. New York. '64.

Buell, Bradley and others. Community planning for human services. Columbia University Press. New York. '52.

Butler, G. D. Introduction to community recreation. 3d ed. McGraw. New York. '59.

Butler, J. A. V. Science and human life. Basic Books. New York. '57.

Cameron, Jenks. Park service; its history, activities, and organization. Johns Hopkins University Press. Baltimore. '22.

*Carlson, R. E. and others. Recreation in American life. Wadsworth. Belmont, Calif. '63.

Chambers, M. M. Youth-serving organizations: national nongovernmental associations; prepared for the Committee on Youth Problems. 3d ed. American Council on Education. Washington, D.C. '48.

Charlesworth, J. C. ed. Leisure in America: blessing or curse? American Academy of Political and Social Science. Philadelphia. '64.

Clark, L. H. ed. Consumer behavior. New York University Press. New York. '54.

Clawson, Marion. Land and water for recreation: opportunities, problems, and policies Rand McNally. Chicago. '63.

Clawson, Marion. Statistics on outdoor recreation. Resources for the Future, Inc. 1145 19th St. Washington 6, D.C. '58.

Colby, Vineta, ed. American culture in the sixties. (Reference Shelf. v 36, no 1) Wilson. New York. '64.

*Corbin, H. D. Recreation leadership. 2d ed. Prentice-Hall. Englewood Cliffs, N.J. '59.

Council of State Governments. States and their older citizens; a summary of the problem of aging in America and a program of action for the states. The Council. 1313 E. 60th St. Chicago 37. '55.

Cozens, F. W. and Stumpf, F. S. Sports in American life. University of Chicago Press. Chicago. '53.

Danford, H. G. Creative leadership in recreation. Allyn. Rockleigh, N.J. '64.

Danford, H. G. Recreation in the American community. Harper. New York. '53.

De Grazia, Sebastian. Of time, work, and leisure. Twentieth Century Fund. New York. '62.

*Denney, Reuel. Astonished muse. University of Chicago Press. Chicago. '57.

Dewhurst, J. F. and others. America's needs and resources: a new survey. Twentieth Century Fund. New York. '55.

Dexter, L. A. and White, D. M. eds. People, society, and mass communications. Free Press. New York. '64.

Dobriner, William, ed. Suburban community. Putnam. New York. '58.

Donahue, W. T. and others, eds. Free time; challenge to later maturity. University of Michigan Press. Ann Arbor. '58.

Duffus, R. L. Adventure in retirement. Norton. New York. '65.

Durant, Henry. Problem of leisure. Routledge. London. '38.

Erikson, E. H. Childhood and society. Norton. New York. '50.

Fenichel, Otto. Collected papers. Norton. New York. '53.

Fisk, G. Leisure spending-behavior. University of Pennsylvania. Philadelphia. '63.

Freud, Sigmund. Beyond the pleasure principle. Bantam. n.d.

Friedmann, E. A. and others. Meaning of work and retirement. University of Chicago Press. Chicago. '54.

Goldner, William. Hours of work. Institute of Industrial Relations, University of California. Berkeley. '52.

Goodman, Paul. Growing up absurd; problems of youth in the organized system. Random House. New York. '60.

Goodman, Paul and Goodman, Percival. Communitas. University of Chicago Press. Chicago. '49.

Green, A. W. Sociology: an analysis of life in modern society. 2d ed. McGraw. New York. '56.

Greenbie, Sydney. Leisure for living. Stewart. New York. '40.

Groombridge, Brian. Education and retirement. National Institute of Adult Education. London. '60.

Gunther, Max. Weekenders. Lippincott. Philadelphia. '64.

Hartley, R. E. and others. Understanding children's play. Columbia University Press. New York. '52.

Hatt, P. K. and Reiss, A. J. Jr. eds. Reader in urban sociology. Free Press. Chicago. '51.

Havighurst, R. J. and Albrecht, Ruth. Older people. Longmans. New York. '53.

Hutchinson, J. L. Principles of recreation. Barnes. New York. '51.

*Johnson, L. B. Campaign statement, Portland, Oregon, September 17, 1964. mimeo. Office of the White House Press Secretary. Washington, D.C. '64.

Kaplan, Max. Leisure in America: a social inquiry. Wiley. New York. '60.

Kleemeier, R. W. ed. Aging and leisure. Oxford University Press. New York. '61.

Kraus, R. G. Recreation leader's handbook. McGraw. New York. '55.

Kreps, J. M. ed. Employment, income, and retirement problems of the aged. Duke University Press. Durham, N.C. '63.

Kubie, S. H. and Landau, Gertrude. Group work with the aged. International Universities Press. New York. '53.

Kutner, Bernard and others. Five hundred over sixty; a community survey on aging. Russell Sage. New York. '56.

Landsberg, H. H. and others. Resources in America's future; patterns of requirements and availabilities, 1960-2000. Johns Hopkins University Press. Baltimore. '63.

Lang, G. E. ed. Old age in America (Reference Shelf. v 33 no 5) Wilson. New York. '61.

Langton, C. V. and others. Principles of health, physical education, and recreation. Ronald. New York. '62.

Larrabee, Eric and Meyersohn, Rolf, eds. Mass leisure. Free Press. Glencoe, Ill. '58.

*Lazazrus, Ralph. Inventing the future; address before biennial meeting of Family Service Association of America, San Francisco, November 16, 1963. Federated Department Stores. 222 W. Seventh St. Cincinnati, Ohio.

Lee, Robert. Religion and leisure in America: a study in four dimensions. Abingdon. Nashville. '64.

Leuchtenberg, William. Perils of prosperity, 1914-32. University of Chicago Press. Chicago. '58.

Leydet, François. Time and the river flowing; Grand Canyon. Sierra Club. San Francisco. '64.

Lobsenz, N. M. Is anybody happy? a study of the American search for pleasure. Doubleday. Garden City, N.Y. '62.

Lucas, Carol. Recreational activity development for the aging in homes, hospitals, and nursing homes. Thomas. Springfield, Ill. '62.

Lundberg, George and others. Leisure; a suburban study. Columbia University Press. New York. '34.

McEntire, Davis. Leisure activities of youth in Berkeley, California. Berkeley Council of Social Welfare and School of Social Welfare, University of California. Berkeley. '52.

MacIver, Robert. Pursuit of happiness; a philosophy for modern living. Simon and Schuster. New York. '55.

McKeown, W. T. ed. Boating in America. Ziff-Davis. New York. '60.

Mannheim, Karl. Freedom, power and democracy. Oxford University Press. New York. '50.

*Maritain, Jacques. Reflections on America. Scribner. New York. '58.

Mayo, Elton. Human problems of an industrial civilization. Viking. New York. '60.

Meyer, H. D. and Brightbill, C. K. Community recreation; a guide to its organization. 3d ed. Prentice-Hall. Englewood Cliffs, N.J. '64.

Meyer, H. D. and Brightbill, C. K. Recreation administration; a guide to its practices. Prentice-Hall. Englewood Cliffs, N.J. '56.

Meyer, H. D. and Brightbill, C. K. State recreation: organization and administration. Barnes. New York. '50.

Michael, Donald. Next generation; prospects ahead for the youth of today and tomorrow. Random House. New York. '63.

*Miller, N. P. and Robinson, D. M. Leisure age: its challenge to recreation. Wadsworth. Belmont, Calif. '63.

*Minow, N. N. Equal time: the private broadcasters and the public interest. Atheneum. New York. '64.

Mitchell, E. D. and Mason, B. S. Theory of play. Barnes. New York. '34.

Morton, J. R. University extension in the United States. University of Alabama Press. University, Ala. '53.

Muir, John. Gentle wilderness; the Sierra Nevada. Sierra Club. San Francisco. '64.

Mulac, M. E. Hobbies: the creative use of leisure. Harper. New York. '59.

Mulac, M. E. Leisure; time for living and retirement. Harper. New York. '61.

Nash, J. B. Philosophy of recreation and leisure. W. C. Brown. Dubuque, Iowa. '60.

National Conference on the Aging. Man and his years; an account of the first National Conference on Aging. Health Publications Institute. Raleigh, N.C. '51.

National Recreation Association. Personnel administration. The association. 8 W. 8th St. New York, N.Y. 10011. '60.

National Recreation Association. Recreation areas, their design and equipment. Prepared by G. D. Butler. 2d ed. Ronald. New York. '58.

National Recreation Congress, 1961. Spotlight on recreation U.S.A. National Recreation Association. 8 W. 8th St. New York, N.Y. 10011. '62.

National Recreation Congress, 1962. Free time, a challenge to free men. National Recreation Association. 8 W. 8th St. New York, N.Y. 10011. '63.

Neumeyer, M. H. Social problems and the changing society. Van Nostrand. Princeton, N.J. '53.

*Neumeyer, M. H. and Neumeyer, E. S. Leisure and recreation; a study of leisure and recreation in their sociological aspects. 3d ed. Ronald. New York. '58.

Olson, Philip, ed. America as a mass society; changing community and identity. Free Press. New York. '63.

Ordway, Samuel. Prosperity beyond tomorrow. Ronald. New York. '56.

Piaget, Jean. Play, dreams and imitation in childhood. Norton. New York. '52.

Pieper, Josef. Leisure, the basis of culture. rev. ed. Pantheon. New York. '64.

Potter, D. M. People of plenty: economic abundance and the American character. University of Chicago Press. Chicago. '54.

Riemer, Svend. Modern city; introduction to urban sociology. Prentice-Hall. Englewood Cliffs, N.J. '52.

Riesman, David. Individualism reconsidered. Free Press. Glencoe, Ill. '54.

Riesman, David and others. Lonely crowd; a study of the changing American character. Yale University Press. New Haven. '50.

Robbins, F. G. Sociology of play, recreation and leisure. W. C. Brown. Dubuque, Iowa. '55

Rosenberg, Bernard and White, David, eds. Mass culture; the popular arts in America. Free Press. Glencoe Ill. '57.

Rosenberg, Harold. Anxious object; art today and its audience. Horizon. New York. '64.

Russell, Bertrand. In praise of idleness and other essays. Barnes. New York. '61.

Samuel, H. L. S. Leisure in a democracy. Cambridge University Press. New York. '49.

Sapora, A. V. H. and Mitchell, E. D. Theory of play and recreation. 3d ed. Ronald. New York. '61.

Schlesinger, A. M. Political and social growth of the American people, 1865-1940. 3d ed. Macmillan. New York. '41.

Schlesinger, A. M. Rise of the city, 1878-1898. Macmillan. New York. '33.

Schramm, Wilbur, ed. Mass communication. 2d ed. University of Illinois Press. Urbana. '60.

Schramm, Wilbur and others. Television in the lives of our children. Stanford University Press. Stanford, Calif. '61.

Sheldon, H. D. Older population of the United States. Wiley. New York. '58.

Simnett, W. E. Leisure: how to enjoy it. Allen & Unwin. London. '46.

Slavson, S. R. Recreation and the total personality. Association Press. New York. '46.

Smigel, E. O. ed. Work and leisure; a contemporary social problem. College and University Press. New Haven. '63.

Soule, George. Time for living. Viking. New York. '55.

Staley, Eugene and others, eds. Creating an industrial civilization. Harper. New York. '52.

Stieglitz, Edward. Second forty years. Lippincott. Philadelphia. '46.

Sumner, W. G. Folkways. (Mentor books) New American Library. New York. '60. [First published in 1907]

Sutherland, W. C. Recreation leadership. Bellman. Cambridge, Mass. '57.

*Tilden, Freeman. Fifth essence; an invitation to share in our eternal heritage. National Park Trust Fund Board. Washington, D.C. 20240. '57.

Tilden, Freeman. State parks; their meaning in American life. Knopf. New York. '62.

Toffler, Alvin. Culture consumers; study of art and affluence in America St. Martin's. New York. '64.

Trow, W. C. Recreation and leisure. McGraw. New York. '52.

United States. Congress. House of Representatives. Committee on Interior and Insular Affairs. Federal Water Project Recreation Act; report, March 3, 1964. (H. Report no 1161 to accompany HR 9032) 88th Congress, 2d session. Supt. of Docs. Washington, D.C. 20402. '64.

United States. Department of the Interior. Community recreation and the public domain; the recreation and public purposes act and related laws. Supt. of Docs. Washington, D.C. 20402. '63.

United States. Department of the Interior. Race for inner space; a special report. Supt. of Docs. Washington, D.C. 20402. '64.

United States. Department of the Interior. Bureau of Outdoor Recreation. Federal assistance in outdoor recreation: available to states, their subdivisions, organizations, individuals. (Technical publication no 1) Supt. of Docs. Washington, D.C. 20402. '64.

United States. Department of the Interior. Bureau of Outdoor Recreation. Federal focal point in outdoor recreation. Supt. of Docs. Washington, D.C. 20402. '64.

United States. Department of the Interior. National Park Service. Areas administered by the National Park Service, January 1, 1964. Supt. of Docs. Washington, D.C. 20402. '64.

United States. Department of the Interior. National Park Service. Your National Parks; a brief history. Supt. of Docs. Washington, D.C. 20402. '61.

*United States. Outdoor Recreation Resources Review Commission. Outdoor recreation for America; a report to the President and to the Congress. Supt. of Docs. Washington, D.C. 20402. '62.

United States. Outdoor Recreation Resources Review Commission. Outdoor recreation literature: a survey report. (ORRRC study report 27) Supt. of Docs. Washington, D.C. 20402. '62.

*Veblen, Thorstein. Theory of the leisure class. (Modern Library) Random House. New York. '34. [First published in 1899]

Warner, W. L. and Lunt, P. S. Social life of a modern community. Yale University Press. New Haven. '41.

Webber, I. L. ed. Aging: a current appraisal. University of Florida. Gainesville. '56.

White, V. K. Measuring leisure-time needs. Welfare Federation of Cleveland. Cleveland. '55.

Williams, A. M. Recreation in the senior years. Association Press. New York. '62.

Williams, W. R. Recreation places. Reinhold. New York. '58.

Wood, M. M. Paths of loneliness; the individual isolated in modern society. Columbia University Press. New York. '53.

Wrenn, C. G. and Harley, D. L. Time on their hands. American Council on Education. 1785 Massachusetts Ave. Washington 36, D.C. '41.

PERIODICALS

Adult Education. 14:80-8. Wint. '64. Challenge confronting adult education. W. E. Cotton.

Adult Leadership. 12:261-2+. Mr. '64. Aged: a challenge to education. T. E. Linton; D. L. Spence.

American Federationist. 71:3-8. My. '64. Automation: the impact on jobs and people. R. B. Cooney.

American Forests. 70:32-4+. Ap. '64. Should the outdoors be free? address. W. N. Aspinall.

American Forests. 70:8-11+. Jl. '64. Farm vacations. J. B. Craig.

American Journal of Sociology. 59:301-90. Ja. '54. Aging and retirement. E. W. Burgess, ed.

American Journal of Sociology. 62:541-615. My. '57. Uses of leisure [entire issue].

American Recreation Journal. 1:8-9. Ap. '61. Where we stand: recreation education in American colleges and universities today. H. D. Sessoms.

American Recreation Society Quarterly Bulletin. 5:16. My. '53. Professional maturity. Roy Sorenson.

*Annals of the American Academy of Political and Social Science. 313:1-147. S '57. Recreation in the age of automation. P. F. Douglass and others, eds.

> Reprinted in this book: Pattern of leisure in contemporary American culture. Margaret Mead. p 11-15.

Business Week. p 142-3+. S. 12, '53. Leisured masses.

Business Week. p 54. O. 10, '53. Updates: leisure.

California Recreation News and Previews. 13:cover page. F. '58. Guide for leisure leaders on the space frontier. Paul Douglass.

Changing Times. 13:46. N. '59. Lost art of loafing.

*Changing Times. 18:18-20. My. '64. Spare time? *What* spare time?

*Christian Science Monitor. p 9. Je. 15, '63. Waterfront at the doorstep. W. C. Harvey.

*Daedalus. Spr. '60. Mass culture and mass media [entire issue].

> Also *separate*: Culture for the millions? Mass media in modern society; ed. by Norman Jacobs. Van Nostrand. Princeton. '61.
> Reprinted *in this book*: Sad heart at the supermarket. Randall Jarrell. Daedalus. p 357-72.

Daedalus. Wint. '63. American reading public [entire issue].

*Editorial Research Reports. 2, no 23:917-34. D. 20, '61. Reading boom: books and magazines. H. B. Shaffer.

Editorial Research Reports. 1, no 8:141-60. F. 28, '62. Expansion of educational TV. F. Y. Blumenfeld.

Editorial Research Reports. 1, no 18:337-54. My. 9, '62. Outdoor recreation. H. B. Shaffer.

Editorial Research Reports. 1, no 22:417-36. Je. 13, '62. Shorter hours of work. R. L. Worsnop.

Editorial Research Reports. 1, no 9:161-82. Mr. 4, '64. City beautiful. H. B. Shaffer.

*Esquire. 52:70-2. Jl. '59. Mass leisure class. Paul Goodman.

Geographical Review. 54:203-38. Ap. '64. Perspective on outdoor recreation: a bibliographical survey. R. I. Wolfe.

Library Trends. 10:10-67. Jl. '61. Population trends—prologue to library development. P. M. Hauser and Martin Taitel.

Life. D. 28, '59. Good life [entire issue].

Life. 56:76-80+. F. 14; 84-6+. F. 21, '64. Too much leisure. Ernest Havemann.

> Same *abridged with title*: Leisure, the great American challenge. Reader's Digest. 85:125-8. Ag. '64.

Michigan Librarian. 30:26-8. Mr. '64. Goals, principles and techniques of participation in adult education programs. Franklin Bouwsma.

Nation. 198:140-4. F. 10, '64. Manpower revolution: a call for debate. G. G. Kirstein.

Nation. 200:41-2. Ja. 18, '65. America the beautiful.

National Parks Magazine. 38:16. Je. '64. Assateague seashore.

National Parks Magazine. 38:16. Je. '64. Seashore proposal; Cape Lookout National Seashore in North Carolina.

National Parks Magazine. 38:2. Jl. '64. Parks as prologue. A. W. Smith.

National Parks Magazine. 38:4-7+. Jl. '64. Indiana Dunes National Lakeshore. Frederic Sicher.

National Resources Journal. 3:250-75. O. '63. Outdoor recreation research: some concepts and suggested areas of study. Marion Clawson and J. L. Knetsch.

National Wildlife. 2:4-7. F.-Mr. '64. Are we running out of outdoors? T. L. Kimball.

*New York Times. Sec. X, p 31+. My. 7, '61. To camp or not to camp.

New York Times. p 95. Ap. 3, '63. Minow seeks law to back N.A.B. code.

*New York Times. p 32. Mr. 24, '64. Man of leisure needs no advice on how to spend his free time. Brooks Atkinson.

New York Times. p 12. Ag. 13, '64. Recreation bill voted by Senate. Nan Robertson.

*New York Times. Sec. X, p 7. S. 13, '64. Motel-hopping across U.S. E. T. Juckett.

New York Times. p 16. Ja. 5, '65. Transcript of the President's message to Congress on the state of the union.

New York Times. p 27. F. 9, '65. Excerpts from Johnson's special message on natural beauty.

New York Times. p 47. F. 9, '65. Everglades National Park is a paradise for fishing, bird and nature buffs. Oscar Godbout.

New York Times Magazine. p 12+. D. 27, '53. New breed of hobbyhorse. Eric Larrabee.

New York Times Magazine. p 12. Ja. 26, '58. Myth of the new leisure class. David Dempsey.

*New York Times Magazine. p 18-19+. Ap. 26, '64. Using our leisure is no easy job. Bruce Bliven.

New York Times Magazine. p 38-9. S. 13, '64. "Once lost, never recaptured." S. L. Udall.

*New York Times Magazine. p 96+. S. 13, '64. Je-ne-sais-quoits or horseshoes? Arnold Hano.

*New York Times Magazine. p 18-19+. D. 20, '64. Ex-national sport looks to its image. Leonard Koppett.

New York Times Magazine. p 26-7+. Ja. 10, '65. Automation is not the villain. P. F. Drucker.

New York Times Magazine. p 12-13+. Ja. 31, '65. Arithmetic of delinquency. Julius Horwitz.

New York Times Magazine. p 68+ Mr. 7, '65. Road to camp right. P. L. Levin.

Newsweek. 65:73-8+. Ja. 25, '65. Challenge of automation.

Pacific Northwest Library Association Quarterly. 28:173-82. Ap. '64. Adult education, a conservative view. Frederick Feringer.

Pacific Northwest Library Association Quarterly. 28:242-4. Jl. '64. Problems of small and medium-sized public libraries in adult education programs. A. S. Jacobs.

Pacific Northwest Library Association Quarterly. 28:244-8. Jl. '64. On defining adult education. Norman Braden.

Pennsylvania Library Association Bulletin. 19:17-19. My. '64. Library services to adults: the educational challenge of technological change. M. H. Goldberg.

*Planning and Civic Comment. 29:1-4+. D. '63; 30:1-4+. Mr. '64. Conservation challenge of the sixties; Horace M. Albright Lecture, University of California, Berkeley, April 19, 1963. S. L. Udall.

Planning and Civic Comment. 30:5-8. Mr. '64. Our outdoor heritage— what we are doing to preserve it. L. S. Rockefeller.

Reader's Digest. 85:148-53. Jl. '64. Stephen Mather, master of the wilderness. D. C. and L. R. Peattie.

*Reader's Digest. 85:161-6+. Ag. '64. Conservation is everybody's battle. J. N. Miller.
   Abridged from To save the landscape. National Civic Review. 53:354-9+. Jl. '64.

Recreation. 44:331-3. N. 3, '50. Community education and recreation. J. F. Regan.

Recreation. 56:278-81. Je. '63. Public recreation: progress and problems. Arthur Todd.

Recreation. 56:401-2. N. '63. Our new automated world. David Gray.

Recreation. 57:9-10. Ja. '64. Leisure, its meaning and implications. Robert Theobald.

Recreation. 57:228-9. My. '64. How active are they?

Recreation. 57:234-5. My. '64. Creative magic for the senior citizen. S. W. Gross.

Recreation. 57:270-1. Je. '64. Policy for county parks and recreation.

Recreation. 57:272-4. Je. '64. State parks recreation menu; Kentucky state parks. W. H. Radke.

*Recreation. 57:276-8. Je. '64. Small watershed projects. H. R. Williams.

*Recreation. 57:280-1. Je. '64. Sports fitness camps. Dorothea Graham.

Recreation. 57:299+. Je. '64. Family campus on the mountaintop.

Recreation. 57:300-1. Je. '64. Action for aging. Mrs. Carter Clopton.

Recreation. 57:318-19. Je. '64. Student approach to recruitment; high-school students. T. M. Kavadas.

Saturday Review. 47:20. Ja. 18. '64. Hail automation, hail peace. Norman Cousins.

Senior Scholastic. 84:11-12+. My. 1, '64. Spare time; America's wasted resource?

Social Forces. 42:112-15. O. '63. Analysis of selected variables affecting outdoor recreation patterns. H. D. Sessoms.

Sociological Review. 12:73-89. Mr. '64. Notes on the concepts of play and leisure. Anthony Giddens.

Successful Farming. 62:42. Ag. '64. Recreation farming; how's it doing? Bill Brantley.

Twentieth Century. 159:493-500. My. '56. Psycho-pathology in industrial life. Elliott Jaques.

Vital Speeches of the Day. 30:636-40. Ag. 1, '64. Cybernated era. Robert Theobald.

Wall Street Journal. 163:1+. My. 7, '64. Mom's a co-ed. F. C. Klein.